SPEAKING OF LOVE

Kierkegaard's Plan for Faith

C. Edward Deyton

UNIVERSITY
PRESS OF
AMERICA

LANHAM • NEW YORK • LONDON

Copyright © 1986 by

University Press of America,® Inc.

4720 Boston Way
Lanham, MD 20706

3 Henrietta Street
London WC2E 8LU England

Library of Congress Cataloging in Publication Data

Deyton, C. Edward, 1943-
    Speaking of love.

    Includes bibliographies.
    1. Kierkegaard, Søren, 1813-1855—Contributions in
the concept of love.   2. Love—History—19th century.
I. Title.
B4378.L6D49   1986   241'.4   86-13187
ISBN 0-8191-5503-9 (alk., paper)
ISBN 0-8191-5504-7 (pbk. : alk. paper)

All University Press of America books are produced on acid-free
paper which exceeds the minimum standards set by the National
Historical Publications and Records Commission.

TABLE OF CONTENTS

Preliminary Gulp

A special obligation is imposed on those who would mine from the rich veins of understanding in the works of Kierkegaard. Few things would have offended him more than to become the occasion for "speculation" rather than personal decision on discipleship to Christ.

If this work is not to be anti-Kierkegaardian, it must aim to sharpen the understanding of love in the Christian context, to eliminate those invalid objections which distract the reader from Kierkegaard's purpose, and to intensify the challenge of Christian love.

An edifying discourse about love presupposes that men know essentially what love is and seeks to win them to it, to move them. But this is in fact not the case. Therefore the 'reflections' must first fetch them up out of the cellar, call to them, turn their comfortable way of thinking topsy-turvy with the dialectic of truth. --from Soren Kierkegaard, Papirer VIII (Kobenhaven: Gyldendalske Boghandel, 1909-1948), A294, translated in Soren Kierkegaard, Works of Love, trans. Howard and Edna Hong (New York: Harper and Row, 1962), p. 12.

Introduction

Kierkegaard's Passion

Kierkegaard not only wrote about paradox: he <u>was</u> a paradox. Copenhagen knew him as something of a dandy, highly visible at the theater, available to waste time in frivolous conversation with anyone, and quite capable of the writings which he published under a pseudonym rather than his own name.

Yet, ironically, Copenhagen would not have expected the highly serious <u>Edifying</u> <u>Discourses</u> of such a person, and these Kierkegaard published under <u>his</u> <u>own</u> <u>name</u>. People were forced to ask: why is the serious work acknowledged by the dandy, while writing more congenial to his image was attributed to a pseudonym?

It is well-known that Kierkegaard offered a schema of three levels of existence, the aesthetic, the ethical, and the religious. But it is far less well recognized that he <u>systematically</u> <u>critiqued</u> <u>each</u> <u>level</u> <u>from</u> <u>its</u> <u>own</u> <u>viewpoint</u> <u>and</u> <u>that</u> <u>of</u> <u>the</u> <u>other</u> <u>levels</u>, using the themes of faith and love. Thus the faith and love of one of the aesthetic level seems a certain way to another aesthete, but a different way to one on the ethical level. The love and faith of one on the ethical level would look a certain way to another on that level, but different to an aesthete. And the same differentiations would apply on the religious level. Through the interplay of these two themes, Kierkegaard carried out his life's strategy, a strategy which is only comprehensible when seen with reference to these themes and how they relate on the various levels of existence.

Kierkegaard's great goal and life passion was to introduce the possibility of authentic Christian faith into Christendom, that officially Christian society with its state-supported church, where everyone is presumed to be a Christian.

Christendom is composed of

People who perhaps never once enter a church, never think about God, never mention His name except in oaths! People upon whom it has never dawned that they might have any obligation to God, people who either regard it as a maxim to be guiltless of transgressing the criminal law, or do not count even this quite necessary! Yet all these people, even those who assert that no God exists, are all of them Christians, call themselves Christians, are recognized as Christians by the State, are buried as Christians by the Church, are certified as Christians for eternity! (1)

The equation or even association of Christianity with Christendom as it is described above is for Kierkegaard a monstrous illusion and an obstacle to true faith. It lulls people into false security, avoiding the necessity of decision. It obscures the categories and issues by which one understands oneself in relation to God.

Another way that Kierkegaard stated his case against Christendom was by way of complaining that the age in which he lived lacked passion:

Our age is essentially one of understanding and reflection, without passion, momentarily bursting into enthusiasm, and shrewdly relapsing into repose. (2)

The same complaint is lodged by Kierkegaard's pseudonum "A" in Volume I of Either/Or, though from a different perspective and for different reasons.(3)

In part Kierkegaard blamed what he called reflection for this lack of passion. Rather than deciding to act, people are willing simply to reflect on life, and if anything does come of the reflective process, it is merely enthusiasm, lacking the inner resolve to carry through a decision.

This reflective and passionless approach to life, according to Kierkegaard, is supported by Hegelian idealism, the prevailing philosophy of the day. Rather than lead people to that consciousness of self and God out of which authentic decision can be made, Hegelianism philosophizes about self-consciousness, and fits every piece of human experience into its system. Philosophical endeavor becomes purely passive; the goal being not authentic decision and action but the fitting of the last pieces of history into the puzzle.

A passionate tumultuous age will overthrow everything, pull everything down; but a revolutionary age (the age of Kierkegaard), that is at the same time reflective and passionless, transforms that expression of strength into a feat of dialectics: it leaves everything standing but cunningly empties it of significance. (4)

Kierkegaard's attack on the Hegelian system and its adherents is to be seen, then, in light of the goal of introducing the possibility of authentic Christianity into Christendom. An age that lacks the possibility of passion is an age without faith, for faith is the highest passion.(5)

Kierkegaard's authorship, and his life as it is inextricably related to his authorship, are an attack upon this illusion of Christendom. But for this attack, Kierkegaard invented "an entirely new military science permeated through and through by reflection,"(6) (although reflection would have a far different goal from reflection in the Hegelian system). It was impossible to

2

conquer the illusion by direct attack: people who believe that they are already Christians simply ignore or avoid the direct campaign, or build other defenses.

No, an illusion can never be destroyed directly, and only by indirect means can it be radically removed. If it is an illusion that all are Christians--and if there is anything to be done about it, it must be done indirectly, not by one who vociferously proclaims himself an extraordinary Christian, but by one who, better instructed, is ready to declare that he is not a Christian at all. That is, one must approach from behind the person who is under the illusion. Instead of wishing to have the advantage of being oneself that rare thing, a Christian, one must let the prospective captive enjoy the advantage of being the Christian, and for one's own part have resignation enough to be the one who is far behind him--otherwise one will certainly not get the man out of his illusion, a thing which is difficult enough in any case. (7)

The attack must begin then, with the categories and concepts which form the self-understanding of the one under illusion. These are aesthetic or ethical categories, and are to be explored by narrative and analysis, causing the one under illusion to become more and more self-conscious. Finally, he or she may reach the point where the wide disparity between the aesthetic or ethical life and authentic Christian faith appears, and with that disparity the possibility of faith.

To become a Christian in Christendom means either to become what one is (the inwardness of reflection or to become inward through reflection), or it means that the first thing is to be disengaged from the toils of one's illusions which again is a reflective modification. (8)

Simply becoming reflective, however, is not the same as becoming a Christian. Rather reflection carried on in an inward fashion, according to Kierkegaard, brings to consciousness the aesthetic and ethical categories by which one lives, and offers for the first time the option to choose instead the religious.

For one does not become a Christian by means of reflection, but to become a Christian in reflection means that there is another thing to be rejected; one does not reflect oneself into being a Christian, but one of another thing in order to become a Christian. . . . (9)

All this was intended to raise the question of Christianity without claiming oneself to be a Christian, and thus goad the reader into raising the question as to his or her own commitment. (10) Kierkegaard referred to the reader that he indeed reached as "that individual," for the mass temperament of Christendom was the very thing he fought. Thus the strategy was aimed at coaxing more and more reflection about the inauthentic categories and values out of which one lived, to the point that true decision and commitment to Christ would be possible.

In order to bring his reader individually to this point, Kierkegaard had to find some vital and central part of life which could be contrasted on the aesthetic, ethical, and religious levels. Such a topic would have to be of compelling interest, inextricably bound up with coming to reflective consciousness, and related to the problem of the illusion of Christendom. The topic he picked was love. As we explore the scope of Kierkegaard's treatment of love, we will see how and why he chooses the more familiar passion of love to entice his reader on to the less familiar passion of faith.

It is doubtful that Kierkegaard was ever conscious that the topic of love became for him the way to accomplish his task. Yet the case will be made here that love became the fundamental paradigm to which he had recourse. It will be shown that love in its various forms appears throughout Kierkegaard's work and that it is used as a model to explain his other concepts and terms. It will also be shown that certain criticisms against Kierkegaard are blunted or at least more clearly focused if they take account of the paradigm of love.

Categories in the Study of Love

As we explore Kierkegaard's notions of love, we will need a set of coherent categories through which to bring the theological traditions of Christianity to bear on his work. Robert Hazo, in conjunction with the Institute of Philosophical Research, has surveyed the idea of human love as it occurs in western culture. He offers us in The Idea of Love (11) a set of concepts of human love which will be outlined below. Although Hazo's study might be considered definitive and exhausitve, it does not need to be defended as such for our purposes. It will be used heuristically, to elucidate the variety of kinds of love in Kierkegaard and show their relationship to the concept of love in other thinkers.

Love is primarily considered as either "tendency" or "judgment." By "tendency" Hazo means an inclination to purposeful action.

Within the restricted sphere of human relationships, tendency in its most genereal sense covers every human inclination that moves or impels one human being to act in a certain way toward others. Such tendencies may take the form of conscious desires, emotional impulses, or deliberate choices; they may also be nothing more than instinctive needs or subconscious yearnings. (12)

Most authors or thinkers consider love to be a tendency; all but a few go beyond love as a general tendency to indicate what the tendency is toward and who is the objective of the tendency called love.

First, love as tendency may be understood as acquisitive desire, the goal being to obtain some good for the self. For some thinkers this is mixed with giving in order to secure the final aim of receiving. For others love as simple acquisitive desire is the tendency to get without giving.

4

An example of love as simple acquisitive desire is found in Plato's Symposium, where Socrates argues that love always involves a deficiency in the lover, and that love is the tendency to overcome the deficiency. (13) Indeed it is through acquisitive love that humans are led from desire of the temporary and physical to desire and contemplation of the ideal. Simple acquisitive desire is directed at things more often than at people.

Mixed acquisitive desire also aims at getting, but involves giving in order to receive. It is to be distinguished from benevolent desire (described below) in that the final aim is always receiving, not giving. In Aristotle's discussion of friendship as reciprocal love among humans, he distinguishes between friendships of virtue, pleasure, and utility. The first aims toward the good of the other; the latter aim for the good of the self:

In the friendship of pleasure and utility, wishing the other well is also present. What distinguishes them from the true friendship of virtue is that the giving involved is always and only present for the sake of getting. (14)

Thus the friendship of pleasure and utility are forms of mixed acquisitive desire.

Benevolent desire has the aim of enhancing the well being of another person or persons. It is an ongoing debate as to whether such is really possible in human love, with some contending that what appears to be benevolent desire is really only a subtle form of mixed acquisitive desire. Among those who hold for its existence, two forms of benevolence may be distinguished. If benevolent desire aims primarily but not exclusively for the good of the other, including also a good for the self, it may be called self-interested benevolence. This is contrasted with mixed acquisitive desire, where the goal is to receive by way of giving. Benevolence and acquisitive desire are mutually exclusive with respect to a particular tendency, i.e., an inclination to act.

Self-interested benevolence may have as its goal for the self satisfaction, moral improvement, mutuality, recognition, and sharing. These, however, only accompany the primary intention, which is a good for the other. Aristotle's friendship of virtue mentioned above is a good example.(15)

Disinterested benevolence desires no return for the self and is characterized by a higher level of awareness and intentionality. Most authors deny the possibility of disinterested benevolence without supernatural aid, de Rougemont and Nygren being contemporary examples. (16)

To summarize what we covered thus far, love may be considered as a tendency, i.e., an inclination to action which is viewed as a good. Acquisitive desire, aiming finally to receive a good, may be simple or may be mixed, the latter aiming to receive through giving. Benevolent desire, aiming finally to give a good, may be self-interested benevolence, where the secondary aim is satisfaction, moral improvement, mutuality, recognition, or sharing of the self, or it may be disinterested, with the exclusive aim of giving. Two other categories of tendential love remain.

Love as sexual desire has its most notable proponent in Sigmund Freud. But Hazo defines sexual desire as

> any yearning the fulfillment of which involves gential pleasures achieved through contact between members of the opposite or the same sex. (17)

Thus, though Freudian theory could point out how many desires are rooted in sexuality, if they lead away from and not toward physical pleasure, they are not considered sexual in this study. Given the workings of the unconscious mind and the ability of any object to become symbolically sexual, however, a case could be argued that all desire is ultimately sexual.

Finally, love as tendency can take the form of desire for union--the inclination of one human to be with and relate to another. The desired union may be one of complementarity or of similarity. In the former, two or more come together to complete the deficiencies in each other and make a whole. The desire may be acquisitive, with the person desiring to complete himself or herself through another, or it may be benevolent, with the person desiring to fulfill the other. Aristophanes' myth of the origin of human beings in Plato's Symposium is probably the best known example of love as the acquisitive desire of complementarity. (18) In the union of similarity the person seeks the other, not as "another half" but as "another self." Aristotle's friends of virtue have "one soul but two bodies." (19)

The second major category of love is "judgment." In love as judgment, cognitive notions become determinative and love expresses the idea of worth. Judgment may be seen as esteem or valuation.

In esteem, someone may be considered to be "good in himself or herself." The esteem may be admiration due to the exceptional nature of the other, or it may be respect of the worth of the other who is not necessarily exceptional. Esteem does not necessarily imply desire. Descartes' notion of an intellectual love that crowns bodily based tendential love is one account of esteem in the literature of love. (20) Esteem, an approving judgment, occurs

> when our souls, perceiving some good, whether it is present or absent, which is suitable (convenable) to it, joins itself voluntarily to that thing; that is to say, the soul considers itself with that good to be a whole of which it is one part and the good the other. (21)

Another kind of love understood as judgment is seen in what Hazo calls "valuation," a judgment which elicts desire. It differs from acquisitive or benevolent desire in that a cognitive, evaluative judgment, not a tendency, gives rise to the desire. Descartes also illustrates this kind of love when speaking of the intellectual love which wills to join itself to the beloved. (22)

6

In his survey Hazo has found that the above categories cover the literature on human love. It should be noted, however, that, while all the notions of love in Hazo fit at least one of the types, some fit into more than one. And some authors, rather than identifying love as limited to one of the categories, include an explicit or implicit typology of love in their own work. Such a one is Søren Kierkegaard.

Hazo's Categories and Traditional Terms for Love

Let us now see how Hazo's categories compare with several well-known terms for love.

Eros is almost always seen as acquisitive desire, whether the object be material or ideal. Plato offers a theory of love as a deficiency in the lover which love seeks acquisitively to overcome. His ladder of eros shows a wide range of beautiful objects toward which love tends. (His notion of the benevolence of a mature thinker for a youth does hold out for the possiblity of a benevolent eros, but this deviates from the basic model of love as a tendency to overcome deficiency. This love, however, may be considered as a desire for the union of similarity.)

Philia, the reciprocal relationship of friends as described by Aristotle, may be acquisitive or benevolent. Acquisitive desire is exemplified by friendship of pleasure or utility, which primarily aims at a good for the lover and secondarily for the beloved. Benevolent desire is seen in the friendship of virtue (for those who are good and alike in virtue), where the beloved is regarded as good in himself. According to Aristotle, only this love is properly called philia, although he himself uses it for the other kinds of friendship as well.

Agape, the New Testament word for love in the Christian context, did not have uniform use by the various authors of the New Testament writings. Paul rarely spoke of agape as human love to God, for he saw agape as spontaneous and unmotivated love. But human love for God is a response to God's love for humanity instead of being spontaneous. Agape, however, is for Paul appropriately predicated of God's love for humanity and the human response to that love in love for others. Agape to Paul was supernatural benevolence and thus opposed to all forms of acquisitive self-love. (23)

For the synoptic gospels and the Johannine literature, there is agreement that agape is supernaturally aided benevolence, but, unlike Paul, it is also possible to have agape for God. The unmotivated spontaniety of agape was not intrinsic to their concept of love. The injunction not to agape the world in I John 2:15 shows that the term is becoming no longer a specific kind of love, but a Christian's love in general, with the issue being which objects are appropriate. It even shows that, when agape is predicated of human love, an acquisitive understanding is possible.

Caritas, as used by St. Augustine, is similar to the use of agape in the synoptic gospels and the Johannine literature. All human love in

Augustine is acquisitive. Humanity is made to seek the highest good. If love channels this seeking upwards to God, it is called caritas; if it is directed downwards toward the world, it is called cupiditas. Augustine also makes the distinction between frui (enjoyment) and uti (use). Caritas correlates with the state where one enjoys God and uses the world; cupiditas correlates with the state where one enjoys the world and uses God.

Kierkegaard's Use of the Danish Words for Love

There are two major roots of words used by Kierkegaard for love and several related terms. We will be assisted in our exploration of these by the Dansk-Englesk Ordbog by Hermann Vinterberg and C.A. Bodelsen, one of the most authoritative Danish-English lexicons, which offers the advantage of containing not only modern but also colloquial and obsolescent meanings. (24)

Elske, verb transitive and intransitive, means to love or adore. Erotic connotations may be included in this love but are not integral to it. Here is a sampling of Kierkegaard's use of the verb elske: speaking of Don Juan he writes, "To see her and to elske her, that was one and the same." (25) In Works of Love Kierkegaard describes our duty to "elske the men we see." (26) Thus elske in Danish is a close equivalent to the English verb "to love," applicable to the same wide variety of types and predicated of the same variety of objects.

The same root may also be used as a noun or adjective. Elskov means love or passion; Elsker is lover; elskelig is lovable. Kierkegaard writes: "Greek elskov, therefore, is psychical, not sensuous. . . . (27) "Chivalrous elskov is also psychical. . . . (28) The duty of love is "to be able to continue finding him elskelig." (29)

Also from the same root, forelske means "to fall in love with" and forelskelse "love affair." Of the Greeks, Kierkegaard writes: "they forelskelse a girl. . . . (30)

The other major Danish word for love is kaerlighed, also spelled kjerlighed. It is a noun readily connected with a wide variety of objects, including country, friends, poetry, etc., but is not used to connote overtly erotic love. Kierkegaard can refer to "Christian kaerlighed," (31) indeed, his work defining the subject is Kjerlighedens Gjerniger.

When drawing an explicit contrast between Christian love and worldly love, Kierkegaard used different roots: "Erotic love (elskov) and friendship (venskab) are preferential and the passion of preference. Christian love (kjerlighed) is self-renunciation's love. . . ." (32) This second root, however, lacks a verb form, and Kierkegaard did not find it inappropriate to use the first as a verb in a religious context: "For to elske God is to elske oneself in truth." (33) Also: "You shall elske your neighbor as yourself." (34) Further, Kierkegaard could speak of "Immature and deceitful kjerlighed," (35) indicating that this root is in no way wholly

8

reserved for positively valued love. Thus we are cautioned to explore the context in which the two roots are used, rather than drawing any automatic distinctions between Kierkegaard's use of them.

Finally, we must mention lidenshab, translated "passion." Kierkegaard does not generally use this in the context of Christian love, but does refer often to faith as a lidenshab, even on occasion as the highest lidenshab.

NOTES

(1) Søren Kierkegaard, The Point of View for My Work As An Author: A Report to History, trans. with introduction by Walter Lowrie, ed. Benjamin Nelson (New York: Harper and Row, 1962), p. 22.

(2) Søren Kierkegaard, The Present Age, trans. Alexander Dru, intro. by Walter Kaufman (New York: Harper and Row, 1962), p. 33.

(3) Søren Kierkegaard, Either/Or I, trans. David and Lillian Swenson (Garden City, New York: Doubleday and Company, 1959), p. 27.

(4) Søren Kierkegaard, The Present Age, p. 42.

(5) Søren Kierkegaard, Fear and Trembling/Sickness Unto Death, trans. with introduction by Walter Lowrie (Garden City, New York: Doubleday and Company, 1954), p. 77.

(6) Søren Kierkegaard, The Point of View for My Work an An Author, p. 38.

(7) Ibid., p. 25.

(8) Ibid., pp. 42, 43.

(9) Ibid., p. 46.

(10) Ibid., p. 18.

(11) Robert Hazo, The Idea of Love, Concepts in Western Thought Series, ed. by Mortimer Adler (New York: Fredrick A. Praeger, Publishers, 1967).

(12) Ibid., p. 16.

(13) Ibid., p. 185.

(14) Ibid., p. 209.

(15) Ibid., p. 210.

(16) Ibid., p. 129.

(17) Ibid., p. 30.

(18) Ibid., p. 21.

(19) Ibid.

(20) Ibid., p. 433.

(21) Ibid.

(22) Ibid., p. 434.

(23) Anders Nygren, Agape and Eros, trans. Philip Watson (Philadelphia, Pennsylvania: The Westminster Press, 1953), pp. 123, 124.

(24) Hermann Vinterberg and C.A. Bodelsen, Dansk-Engelsk Ordbog (Kobenhavn: Gyldendalske Boghandel, 1954).

(25) Søren Kierkegaard, Either/Or I, p. 93.

(26) Søren Kierkegaard, Works of Love, trans. Howard and Edna Hong (New York: Harper and Row, 1964), p. 158.

(27) Søren Kierkegaard, Either/Or I, p. 92.

(28) Ibid., p. 93.

(29) Søren Kierkegaard, Works of Love, p. 158.

(30) Søren Kierkegaard, Either/Or I, p. 29.

(31) Søren Kierkegaard, Works of Love, p. 105.

(32) Ibid., p. 65.

(33) Ibid., p. 113.

(34) Ibid., p. 29.

(35) Søren Kierkegaard, Fear and Trembling/Sickness Unto Death, p. 131.

Chapter I
Aesthetic Love
Aesthetically Considered

Love and the Levels of Existence

The Kierkegaardian formulation that has received perhaps the highest attention and acceptance is the notion of three qualitatively distinct levels of existence: the aesthetic, ethical, and the religious.

Kierkegaard's title Stages on Life's Way should not lead us to assume that the levels are in a progression, or that they are related to aging or any other of life's natural or inevitable movements. Nor should we assume that all of the concerns and characteristics of one level are left behind in movement to another: many are brought along, though qualitatively changed. For this reason scholars such as James Collins prefer "spheres of existence" to "stages," showing how aesthetic, ethical, and religious existence overlap on areas of life common to them all. (1) Having noted this aspect of Kierkegaard's formulation, however, we will use the metaphor of "level" to elucidate Kierkegaard's own valuing of aesthetic, ethical, and religious existence. For Kierkegaard did not present these as equal in worth. Rather that ethical is higher than the aesthetic and the religious is above them both. Indeed it could be argued that the metaphor of "stage" is the way the ethical pseudonym Hilarius Bookbinder understands the relation between them on a psycho-social model, whereas "level" may be closer to Kierkegaard's own understanding. Kierkegaard himself was at pains to distinguish the structures of existence which he posited from a natural, developmental model which "stadier" could connote. Therefore, his own references were most often to "the aesthetic," "the ethical," or "the religious." We conclude that we would do Kierkegaard no disservice by avoiding the notion of "stage" in favor of "level," which connotes the value structure which Kierkegaard espoused.

Much attention has been paid to the characteristics of life as it is lived on each of the levels, and the placement of the various Kierkegaardian pseydonyms and persona. We shall draw upon that work rather than duplicate it, for our goal is to see how love is related to each of the three levels and how it serves as a catalyst in the movement between them.

Two crucial ways Kierkegaard compared the levels of existence were by the qualities of self-consciousness and will, as connoted by the terms "dread" and "despair" respectively. These terms have as their background Kierkegaard's view of the self as a relationship which, when actualized, is also spirit.

> The self is a relationship which relates itself to its own self, or it is that in the relation (which accounts for it) that the relation relates itself to its own self; the self is not the relation but (consists in the fact) that the relation relates itself to its own self. Man is a synthesis of the infinite and the finite, of the temporal and the eternal, of freedom and necessity, in short it is synthesis. (2)

But this self as relationship is spirit when it relates itself consciously and by act of will to God, the one who constitutes it.

> This formula (i.e. that the self is constituted by another) is the expression for the total dependence of the relation (the self namely), the expression for the fact that the self cannot of itself attain and remain in equilibrium and rest by itself, but only by relating itself to that Power which constitutes the whole relation. (3)

When the self does not relate to itself and to its constitutive Power by a conscious act of will, it is said to be in dread/dispair. Although used at times almost interchangeably, "dread" indicates in its degree the level of self-consciousness of the person, and "despair" the accompanying degree of willingness to accept responsibility for one's self. Dread is the state of anticipation just prior to the recognition by the self of its makeup and its alienation from the Power that constitutes it. It is, from a psychological (aesthetic) point of view, a "sympathetic antipathy and an antipathetic sympathy." (4)

> Everything turns upon dread coming into view. Man is a synthesis of the soulish and the bodily. But a synthesis is unthinkable if the two are not united in a third factor. . . . (In innocence) the spirit is present, but in a state of immediacy, a dreaming state. (5)

This "coming into view" of dread is the element of consciousness that characterizes the self as it realizes its dialectical nature.

> Despair is defined as

> the relationship in a relation which relates itself to itself. . . this thing of despairing is inherent in man himself; but if he were not a synthesis, he could not despair, neither could he despair if the synthesis were not originally from God's hand in the right relationship. (6)

The pseudonym Anti-Climacus, very close to speaking for Kierkegaard himself, then goes on to explore despair as a category of will, for it is possible either to despair by failing to will to be oneself or by willing despairingly to be oneself. Nor does one have to be aware of the disrelationship in order to be in despair, and therein is the correlation with the term "dread":

> So then, the fact that the man in despair is unaware that his condition is despair, has nothing to do with the case, he is in despair all the same. If despair is bewilderment (Forvildelse), then the fact that one is unconscious of it is the additional aggravation of being at the same time under a delusion (Vildfarelse). Unconsciousness of despair is like unconsciousness of dread (cf. The Concept of Dread by Vigilius Haufniensis): the dread characteristic of spiritlessness is recognizable precisely by the spiritless sense of security; but never-the-less dread is at the bottom of it. . . . The despairing man who is unconscious of being in despair is, in comparison with him who is conscious of it, merely a negative step further from the truth and from salvation. (7)

As we will see, Kierkegaard's pseydonyms use the metaphor of depth equivocally with these terms, at times referring to the person at the lowest level of self-consciousness and self-willing as being "deep" in dread/despair, while at other times referring to those persons poised at the boundary line between levels of existence as being in their intensity "deeper" in despair/dread.

Since it was Kierkegaard's goal to enable his reader to move beyond the bounds of his or her present level of existence and into truly religious experience, he examined the various levels from the perspective of each other. To one on the aesthetic level, he showed how the ethical and the religious would appear. To one on the ethical level, he showed how the aesthetic and the religious would appear. And since the topic of love pervades Kierkegaard's writings, it is treated from all of these perspectives. Thus we are provided with a convenient format for exploring Kierkegaard's work, which also enables us to respect his request that the pseydonyms be treated as distinct perspectives. Accordingly we will see how Kierkegaard portrayed aesthetic love's self-understanding and its understanding of love on the aesthetic and religious levels. And finally, we will see religious love's self-understanding and its understanding of aesthetic and ethical love.

The Aesthetic Level of Existence

The work of Hegel was a great influence on Kierkegaard's notion of levels of existence, although finally most of Hegel was rejected. In The Phenomenology of Spirit Hegel presented a series of dialectically related stages of life in which the mind moves from lack of self-consciousness through consciousness of self, the universal, and the absolute. Kierkegaard radically differed with Hegel, however, by picturing the transition between the levels as an act of will rather than an act of mind. And, indeed, he continued to view all of Hegel's philosophy as principally an expression of the first level because it lacked the category of will necessary to move onward.

13

The aesthetic level is characterized by sensation, impulse, and emotion, exhibiting many of the values so central to the Romantic movement:

Sensitive, emotional, preferring color to form, the exotic to the familiar, eager for novelty, for adventure, above all for the vicarious adventure of fantasy, reveling in disorder and uncertainty, insistent on the uniqueness of the individual to the point of making a virtue of eccentricity. . . . (8)

Kierkegaard included in the aesthetic level not only those who are immersed in this side of life but also those who are aware enough to articulate and defend these characteristics as values, just as the Romantic movement embraced not only those who gloried in experience, fantasy, and imagination, but also those who presented and defended this as a viable option. At the lowest level of the aesthetic life, from Kierkegaard's view, are the former, whose experience is so immediate, i.e., unmediated by reason and self-consciousness, that there would be no possibility for articulation. Above and just short of the act of decision necessary to move out of the aesthetic level are the essayists, poets, and diarists who attempt to understand the aesthetic life from within. We will review in this order some of the stories of love in Kierkegaard's writings.

Love and Lowest Immediacy

In an appreciation of the music of Mozart, "A," the pseydonymous author of the first section of Either/Or, explores the dawning of self-consciousness through love. The lowest level is represented by the page in Figaro. In the page

The sensuous awakens, not yet to movement, but to a hushed tranquility; not to joy and gladness, but to a deep melancholy. Desire is not yet awake, it is only a gloomy foreboding. (9)

In the page desire does not really focus on its object. Mozart's music expresses for him love as an intoxication, moving not toward "the transprent joy of life" but remaining in a melancholy dream of "unclarified gloom." (10)

A slightly higher level of consciousness is represented by Papageno in The Magic Flute. Papageno is bubbly with love, which is here awake and seeking an object, and yet self-consciousness is not sufficiently developed to become aware of oneself as desiring. What is taking place in Papageno's love is not acquisitive desire in the full sense. Rather his love is a general tendency to reach out, to explore, to discover. (11)

Stories of Seduction and Broken Engagement

The stories examined below are combined into one section because they contain interlocking elements and because they show the movement of self-consciousness as love leads to the boundary of aesthetic life. Although Kierkegaard is highly innovative in the way he composed or recast these stories, the idea of seduction as a conscious and deliberate activity, as well as the form of the epistolary novel was explored prior to him by Choderlos de Laclos in Les Liasons Dangereuses. Although it cannot be proved that Kierkegaard read Laclos, it is likely, and this may have been the origin of his explorations of love, seduction, and self-consciousness. (12)

In Either/Or, "A" continues his essay on Mozart, praising him with great feeling for allowing, more than any other composer, the element of the sensuous to flow through his music. In Mozart's version of the Don Juan tales, Don Giovanni (the Italian rendering of the name) is portrayed as a reckless libertine. After an amorous relationship with Donna Anna, he is seeking to free himself from her when her father interrupts and a duel is fought. Her father, the Commendatore of the area, is killed.

Don Giovanni continues his search for conquests, but stumbles across Donna Elivira, whom he has already seduced and who is longing for him still. Leaving his servant, Leporello, to explain his desertion, Don Giovanni moves on, joining a group of merry peasants. Here he attempts to seduce Zerlina, but Donna Elvira interrupts, denouncing him.

Later Don Giovanni hears the voice of the Commendatore speaking to him in a graveyard through his memorial statue. He boldly invites the statue to dinner. To his shock, the statue appears, seizes Don Giovanni by the hand, and drags him unrepentant to hell.

In "A's" review of Don Juan, he does not stop to tell the full story of the opera. Rather he prefers to deal with the seduction and rejection of Donna Elvira, alluding to the rest of the story. What is significant for us is the analysis which is interwoven with the fragmentary appreciation. According to "A," Don Juan's love is "desire absolutely determined as desire; . . . . desire is absolutely sound, victorious, triumphant, irrestible, and dae- monic." (13) "To see her and to love her, that was one and the same." (14)

Yet "A" calls into question whether Don Juan can really be con- sidered a seducer:

> To be a seducer requires a certain amount of reflection and con-
> sciousness, and as soon as this is present, then it is proper to speak of
> cunning and intrigue and crafty plans. This consciousness is lacking in
> Don Juan. Therefore, he does not seduce. He desires and this desire
> acts seductively. To that extent he seduces. He enjoys the
> satisfaction of desire; as soon as he has enjoyed it he seeks new
> object, and so on endlessly. (15)

Don Juan's love is simple acquisitive desire, yet what he desires is not so much the possession of the particular woman who is the object of his attention. Though he is unconscious of it, he desires simply the experience of the woman. Once this experience is acquired, the desire is satisfied, and

15

the object of his acquisitive love changes. Completing the essay begun with the page in _Figaro_, Don Juan represents the highest of the "immediate stages of the erotic."

In an essay called "Shadowgraphs," "A" relates the love story of Goethe's _Faust_. Faust, professor and scholar, seeks to penetrate to the essence of things, but discovers himself limited even after acquiring magical powers. Mephistopheles strikes a bargain that he will show Faust a wider experience of life if Faust will surrender his soul to him when Faust has reached a moment so beautiful that he would prolong it. (This desire, as we shall see, is one of the major issues for the aesthetic level.)

In the first part of Faust's wider experience of life, Mephistopheles shows him the image of Margaret, an innocent young maiden, in a mirror. He meets her and falls in love. She gives herself to him and becomes pregnant. When her brother discovers the situation, he and Faust fight and the brother is killed. After Faust flees, Margaret becomes demented, drowns the child which she has borne, and is charged with murder. Meanwhile Faust and Mephistopheles are off in revelry. Faust returns and attempts to rescue Margaret, but she refuses and dies. Later in the story she intercedes for Faust's salvation.

Kierkegaard mentions with enthusiasm in his _Journal_ the comparison between Faust and Don Juan as literary figures made by Christian Dietrich Grabbe in _Don Juan and Faust_, (16) but the important issue is how Kierkegaard's pseydonum "A" perceives them:

> Faust is a demonic figure like Don Juan but higher. The sensuous first becomes significant for him only after he has lost an entire preceding world, but the consciousness of his loss is not erased, it is constantly present, and he seeks therefore in the sensuous not so much enjoyment as diversion of mind. (17)

Faust's love is more self-conscious than Don Juan's and more focused: "What he desires is the pure, rich, untroubled, immediate happiness of a woman's soul, but he desires it not spiritually, but sensually." (18) Love for Margaret, then, represents to Faust the immediacy he has lost and longs to participate in again. Yet, unlike Don Juan, Faust finally desires not the woman but the experience of her. Faust's love is another example of simple acquisitive desire, though he is closer to realizing this than Don Juan could ever be.

In the figure of Johannes the Seducer, "A" gives us a look at someone more reflectively demonic than Don Juan or Faust. The aesthete finds a diary in a desk drawer, presumably the same desk drawer mentioned in the beginning of _Either/Or_. The dairy, named "Dairy of the Seducer," contains an account of the seduction of Cordelia Wahl, the last name being fictitious.

The story, extracted from the descriptions of the diary, is that Johannes notices and desires an innocent young maiden, Cordelia. He

16

becomes the confidant of Edward, her suitor, and undermines his suit, thereafter becoming engaged to her.

But Johannes is the self-conscious aesthete, and he reflects:

The curse of an engagement is always on its ethical side. . . . Under the heaven of the aesthetic, everything is light, beautiful, transitory; when the ethical comes along, then everything becomes harsh, angular, infinitely boring. (19)

Johannes skillfully maneuvers Cordelia toward the conviction that she must break off the engagement in order that their love may have freedom to grow. In the countryside he seduces her and then abandons her. But even previous to this he has described himself in the dairy as

. . . an aesthete, an eroticist, one who has understood the nature and meaning of love, who believes in love and knows it from the ground up and only makes the private reservation that no love affair should last more than six months at the most and that every erotic relationship should cease as soon as one has had the ultimate enjoyment. (20)

Johannes has been aware all long of the ultimate goal of the relationship. There has been a savoring, not only of the physical act of seduction, but of the whole process leading up to it. He has even manipulated Cordelia into taking responsibility for the broken engagement. Thus "there could not be the slightest thing to which she could appeal. . . . she must constantly struggle with the doubt as to whether the whole affair was not a figment of the imagination." (21)

Though "A" concludes that Johannes was too intellectual to be a seducer in the common understanding of the word, he nevertheless exhbits love as simple acquisitive desire. What he desired, and was conscious of desiring all along, was a total aesthetic experience, of which the actual physical moment was only the completion. "I seek the immediate. It is the eternal element in love that the individuals first exist for one another in the moment of love." (22)

Yet the immediate is not really possible for a figure as reflective as Johannes. If he were truly immersed in the immediate, he would not set limitations on time or on the experience, but rather would assume that it would last. The closest approximation that Johannes can hope for is the intense savoring of the immediacy of another. For he is self-conscious enough to perceive that he is on the boundary of the ethical level, yet closes himself off from the possibility of commitment and self-revelation. Aesthetic love is for him the retreat from the crisis at the top of the aesthetic level. Just as the victims of seduction are "shipwrecked" between immediacy and reflection, Johannes is frozen in his demonic despair. In contrast to the earlier "Immediate Stages of the Erotic," the seducer is in the non-immediate stage of the erotic, from which there seems little possibility of movement.

In <u>Repetition</u> a young man confides to Constantine Constantious, the psychologist who is another of Kierkegaard's pseydonyms, that he is in love with a woman and that she returns his affection. But his tendency to melancholy asserts itself:

> ... on one of the first days of his engagement, he was capable of recollecting his love. Substantially he was through with the whole relationship. Before he begins he has taken such a terrible stride that he has lept over the whole of life. . . . (23)

By "recollecton" Constantine means the calling to cognition of what is essential and lasting, the act of knowing in the Platonic sense. Rather than experiencing the beauty of the love relationship in its immediacy, the young man has lost the immediacy by melancholy reflection upon it.

The young man is of interest to Constantine because the psychologist is seeking to find out if one can recollect forwards, which he calls "repetition." In other words, can we understand how significant experiences of the present can continue to have lasting importance, or is the immediacy of these experiences lost forever when we reflect upon them? Can the delight of the moment be recaptured in the future? "Repetition" is an attempt to understand aesthetically how the eternal can enter into the moment, and how the tedious onrush of life can be overcome. To the aesthete this means simply the assurance that what is good in the present is not of necessity lost for the future, that it can be repeated. Grace on the aesthetic level would simply be the sense that one is not instantly alienated from what is meaningful in the present, but that it may be recaptured. We will see how on the religious level this reclamation is not a natural possibility, as Constantine imagines, but is made possible by faith.

Constantine defends the correctness of the young man's recollection: "the man who in his experience of love has not experienced it has never loved." (24) But something more was required:

> This potentiated act of recollection is the eternal expression of love at the beginning, it is the token of real love, but on the other hand an iron elasticity is required in order to be able to make use of it. This he lacked, his soul was too soft for it. (25)

The young man disappears without informing his fiancee or Constantine, foiling a plot by the latter to break off the engagement by making the young man appear as a deceiver. After awhile he begins to write Constantine, exploring his life situation through a discussion of Job. He focuses on the fact that Job received double for what he lost. This he calls "repetition," coming about "When all conceivable human certitude and probability pronounced it impossible." (26) The young man writes that he is expecting a "thunderstorm": a repetition that will allow him to become a husband and thus, like Job, receive again that which he had lost.

But he finds that his former fiancee has married. Repetition is spiritual, not temporal; what is restored to him is not the object of his love, but himself.

Constantine writes that the young man has become a poet--one who thinks the universal with passion. The girl has been the occasion to awaken the poet in him. But, Constantine conjectures that

> If he had had a deeper religious background, he would not have become a poet. Then everything would have acquired religious significance. (27)

But this thought is not carried forward. It is left to tantalize us by the author of this psychological experiment, who for his own part, does not even reach beyond the position of observer to become a poet.

In Repetition we have another story of broken engagement to place beside the story of Johannes. But here the broken engagement is not the act of a seducer or a deceiver, but the only alternative for one who understands himself to be truly in love. In this instance love is not simply sensuous as in Don Juan, nor the sensuous desire for the spiritual as in Faust, nor the calculating seduction of the demonic aesthete Johannes. It is the sincere desire of one who nevertheless experiences the impediment to love within himself.

In the story of Agnes and the merman we see the aesthetic at the absolute dialectical turning point. Johannes de silentio provides us with three versions of the story, two of which are useful at this point.

In the first version, the merman shoots up out of the depths to seduce Agnes, who stands gazing down into the mystery of the sea. Agnes is willing to follow him and is lifted into his arms as he prepares to plunge back into the waters. But the absolute innocence of her faith in him arrests his leap.

> Then the merman collapses, he is not able to resist the power of innocence, his native element is unfaithful to him, he cannot seduce Agnes. He leads her back again, he explains to her that he only wanted to show her how beautiful the sea is when it is calm, and Agnes believes him. (28)

Though he has the power to seduce Agnes, he cannot accept her as his prey. The power of innocense has won. But he is not able to be faithful and committed to her, for he is a merman and his love is demoniacal, closed off from being able to give himself to another. As he returns to the sea, it rages about him and despair rages within him.

A second version reverses the roles. The merman is seeking that innocent maiden who, as legend teaches, can deliver him from the misery of his demoniacal loneliness. He falls in love with Agnes and approaches her, not to seduce but to offer himself to her.

> But Agnes was no quiet maiden, she was fond of the roar of the sea, and the sad sighing beside the inland lake pleased her only because she seethed more strongly within. She would be off and away, she

would rush wildly out into the infinite with the merman whom she loved--so she incites the merman. She disdained his humility, now pride awakens. And the sea roars and the waves foam and the merman embraces Agnes and plunges with her into the deep. Never had he been so wild, never so full of desire, for he had hoped by this girl to find deliverance. (29)

At the pinnacle of the demoniacal, the merman had found one as demoniacal as he. Instead of being delivered by love into a fully human existence, he had created a mermaid who seduced men into the sea. As they lost interest in each other, he also lost the opportunity to escape the loneliness of the demonic.

Love and Reflective Grief

Kierkegaard also works with stories which tell of seduction and broken engagement from a passive point of view. In "Shadowgraphs," "A" sketches the stories of three women and their unhappy love. Unlike women who are brought to grief because of the death of the beloved, or some other understanding impediment, and whose grief thus requires not only reflection but simple acceptance, these women are forced to ponder their love for a deceiver.

In Goethe's Clavigo, we read the story of a woman broken by an unhappy love affair. Clavigo is engaged to Marie Beaumarchais but leaves her, and she must struggle not only to deal with her unhappiness, but also to understand why he left. If she were simply hurt or disappointed, she could find repose in her unhappiness and be comforted by those around her. But she must struggle with the question: was Clavigo really a deceiver?

'He was no deceiver; for if he had been, he must have been conscious of being one from the beginning. But this is not so; my heart tells me that he has loved me.' If one insists upon this conception of a deceiver, then it follows in all likelihood that a deceiver has never existed. (30)

Since she cannot really believe that Clavigo was a deceiver, she is cut off from those around her, who have no difficulty regarding him so and encouraging her to do the same. Her grief becomes secret, and the more isolated she becomes, the more her grief can only turn upon itself.

This process of reflection pursues an endless path, and can come to an end only if the individual arbitrarily breaks it off by bringing something else into play, a resolution of the will, but in so doing the individual brings himself under ethical categories, and loses his aesthetic interest. (31)

Marie does not achieve this resolution of the ethical, but the restlessness of her grief will not let her return completely to the comfort of immediacy.

No illusion overshadows her with its quiet coolness while she assi-
miliates the pain. She lost childhood's illusion when she gained that
of love, and she lost love's illusion when Clavigo deceived
her; . . . (32)

In the Kruse adaptation of Don Juan, Donna Elvira has been a nun
prior to her seduction by Don Juan.

The more significant the past she leaves behind her, the more closely
must she cling to him; the more closely she has twined herself about
him, the more terrible becomes her despair when he leaves her. Her
love is even from the beginning a kind of despair; nothing has any
significance for her, either in heaven or on earth, except Don
Juan. (33)

Despite overwhelming evidence, Elvira will not be convinced that
Don Juan is a deceiver. She continues to seek further proof, thus prolonging
her suffering indefinitely. She has no supportive environment, for she has
left the world of the convent to pursue her love. Thus she stands absolutely
alone.

Two possibilities exist. She could return to the cloister, renouncing
her love for Don Juan. But this she cannot do, for she cannot bring herself to
despair totally of her hope for Don Juan. The second possibility is to
continue to pursue him, which is the course she follows. A third possibility,
that of seeking the love of another, is unthinkable. Therefore, her destiny is
to love Don Juan, probably unto death, struggling all the while against the
mounting evidence of his deception.

If I were to imagine a human being in a wreck at sea, unconcerned for
his life, remaining on board because there was something he wanted
to save and yet could not save, because he could not decide what it
was that he should save, then would I have a picture of Elvira; . . . (34)

Faust is shown the image of Margaret in a mirror and he desires her
for her simple pure immediacy. She humbly returns his love but he leaves
her after it is discovered that she is pregnant.

At first sight it might seem that the only difference between Elvira
and Margaret was that which exists between two individuals who have
had the same experience. The difference is, however, far more
essential, not based so much upon the different personalities of the
two women, as upon the essential difference between a Don Juan and
a Faust. (35)

As we have seen in the previous section, Faust was more conscious
of his actions and their intent than Don Juan. "A" has invited us to view the
difference between Margaret and Elvira by reference to their seducers,
treating the quality of their despair as a function of the level of self-
consciousness of Faust and Don Juan. Although Elvira is shipwrecked in her

grief, Margaret has been absolutely frozen by the deception of Faust. Thus neither Elvira nor Margaret is seen by "A" as active in the constitution of their level of self-consciousness. The seducers are the actors, and the responses of the women are basically passive.

In loving Faust, Margaret is broken to pieces, for the figure of Faust is too great for her. She cannot maintain the immediacy which has been her ground and defense, and which Faust so coveted, and he does not wish to take her up into the realms of reflection. And so he abandons her. Margaret can neither go forward reflectively into the possibilty of an ethical and religious existence, for Faust has overpowered her and only he can take her in that direction. Nor can she return to the realms of immediacy, for Faust has carried her irrevocably if reluctantly beyond this. She has no place to go, and dementia is her only escape.

The First Love

In an analytical essay on Scribe's play The First Love, "A" explores the romantic notion that the first love is the only true love. He begins by pointing out at length that every literary production has both inspiration and an occasion, i.e., more or less arbitrary point of departure. The occasion for the writing of this review came about because the aesthete and his first love attended by accident the same performance of The First Love and thereafter romantically vowed to see it every time it was subsequently produced.

The play revolves around the belief of sixteen-year-old Emmeline that "The first love is the true love, and one loves only once." (36) She has vowed love for her cousin Charles, whom she has not seen in eight years. When Rinville decides to marry well (Emmeline's father is wealthy), his suit is rejected by Emmeline even though the father is enthusiastic about him. The father is infuriated at Charles when he learns that the impediment is Emmeline's loyalty to him.

Rinville decides to pose as Charles to win Emmeline's affections, but meanwhile Charles appears, now married, hoping for some monetary support from Emmeline's father. He decides to impersonate Rinville. Thus, in the name of faithfulness to first love, Emmeline provides laughter to audiences by accepting Rinville in the guise of Charles and rejecting Charles in the guise of Rinville. When Emmeline learns that Charles is married, she accepts Rinville to please her father, but states explicitly that she is not marrying for love, since Charles was her first and only true love.

As champion of the absolute validity of first love, Emmeline represents a numerous class of mankind. One thinks indeed that it may be possible to love more than once; but the first love is still essentially different from every other. This cannot be explained in any other way than by assuming that there is a beneficient spirit who has presented mankind with a little gilding with which to embellish life. The proposition that the first love is the true love is very accomodating and can come to the aid of mankind in various ways. If a man is not fortunate enough to get possession of what he desires, then he still has the sweetness of the first love. (37)

Years later "A" met his "first love" again while writing about Scribe's play. She was now engaged to another, and assured him that she had never truly loved him, for her present betrothed was her real "first love." Thus "A" also can testify to the way the concept of "first love" can be manipulated to reinforce the romantic intensity of the aesthetic life.

The power and immediacy of first love has trapped the aesthetic consciousness into assuming that all "true" love must have these characteristics, and this is the assumption which "A" mocks. But he leaves open the question of whether it is possible to recapture what is essential in the first love after second love has necessitated a reflective posture. We have already seen this question explored in Repetition. The aesthetic answer to the question is finally negative. Those who, in the interactions of love, have reached the boundary of the aesthetic, either by acting to break off a love affair, or by suffering passively the rejection by a faithless lover, may not again enter into the Eden of immediate love.

Aesthetic Love's Self-understanding

The aesthetic understanding of aesthetic love is very close to Hazo's category of "tendency," the inclination to act springs from within and from other than cognitive sources. The fascination of love is the quest after the beloved; possession of the beloved is the death of love in its most intense forms, for aesthetic love knows only how to seek.

Simple acquisitive desire characterizes most of the stories we have just reviewed. Possibly love could be classified here as sexual love, at least in the case of Don Juan and Johannes the Seducer. Yet it is important to note that the focus is on the aesthete's experience of consummation and not on the consummation itself. And in the case of the young man in Repetition, the possibility of consummation drives him into retreat. The category of sexual love, then, is not the most adequate one for understanding the stories we have before us.

Only the desire to add to the knowledge and self-consciousness of Cordelia in the story of Johannes the Seducer is the exception to the picture of aesthetic love as simple acquisitive desire. The desire in this instance is for a good for the beloved, though, as with all mixed acquisitive desire, the love is finally self-oriented.

There is a high degree of correlation between Hazo's category of love as tendency and the immediacy of aesthetic love. From the lowest upon itself of Johannes, aesthetic love is antithetical to the cognitive choices of love characterized as judgment. Johannes observes:

Personally I want no histories; I have seen enough of them; I seek the immediate. It is the eternal element in love that the individuals first exist for one another in the moment of love. (38)

Love on the aesthetic level is first of all a tendency to reach out to the beloved, to grasp, to embrace. And there it remains in unreflective happiness until its course is interrupted by the loss of the beloved. Even here the lover will tend to seek another beloved in an unreflective way unless he or she is forced to reflect, as in the case of deception.

Once reflection has brought the person to the boundary of the aesthetic, several options occur. One may step by self-conscious choice into the ethical. Another is to shrink back by avoidance of choice into the aesthetic. (And just as love can be the vehicle to bring one to the boundary of the aesthetic, so it can be used in the attempt to return to immediacy.) Such is the case with the seducers who pour out great energy to be immersed for a few delightful moments in the experience of seduction.

Finally the lover at the aesthetic boundary may not be able to rid himself or herself even for a moment of the tortures of reflection in order to return to immediacy. Such was the case with the women who were frozen in their reflective grief, unable to push on into the ethical, unable to give up their beloved whom they continue to love aesthetically. These options correlate closely with the forms of despair viewed under the aspect of consciousness in The Sickness Unto Death. We will explore this further when we look at how the religious stage views aesthetic love.

The stories "A" and Constantine, of love on the aesthetic level are, in Hazo's terms, highly tendential, involving a non-cognitive source of motivation. Love, except in rare instances, is simple acquisitive desire for the object of love or a delightful experience with the object of love. Yet we may presume that the potential for mixed acquisitive desire is present, that the lover may desire a good for the beloved if only to enhance the lover's experience. There is no question of a qualitative leap in love until we reach the issue of disinterested benevolence, which nowhere appears on the aesthetic level.

Our exploration of the Danish words used for love, undertaken in the Introduction, is borne out on the aesthetic level. Elske and Kjerlighed both appear; the only difference in meaning is that Kjerlighed is generally not used for the more sensual aspects of erotic love. But even this distinction does not always apply, for Johannes the Seducer can reflect:

I am an aesthete, an eroticist, one who has understood the nature and meaning of Kjerlighedens, who believes in Kjerligheden and knows it from the ground up. . . . (39)

The context of the words for love in the stories we have reviewed leads the aesthete to see love on the aesthetic level as eros in varying the boundary of the ethical, aesthetic love desires the beloved for its own good. That good may be sensual delight, erotic pleasure, or an interpersonal relationship. But always, in the accounts of aesthetic love we have reviewed, the acquisitive goal of eros is evident.

As we complete this survey of how the aesthetic writers in Kierkegaard's works view love on their own level, we must note two issues which have received little attention but which nevertheless correlate with love on the aesthetic level.

First, we must explore the relationship between acquisitive desire and the union of complementarity. Although the aesthetic writers do not we should note that in Hazo's categories the desire for union can be combined with acquisitive desire. The lover, feeling a deficiency in the self, seeks to complete himself or herself by union with the beloved. Since several of the figures we have just reviewed have such a sense of deficiency, particularly those at the lowest level of the aesthetic consciousness and those caught up in reflective grief, the survey of aesthetic love should take account of this possibility.

The immediacy of aesthetic love is a drawing close to the beloved in an unreflective way. The lover needs the beloved and feels incomplete without him or her. When the closeness with the beloved is lost, the emptiness prompts reflection and a sense of the awareness of the lack of full selfhood. Thus we see that desire for the beloved was all along the desire to complement oneself and complete one's selfhood. Likewise the seductive impulse of the aesthete, recoiling from the necessity of choice at the boundary of the aesthetic is a desire to recover a lost immediacy through closeness to one whose consciousness is still immediate. Behind the view of love as acquisitive desire in the aesthetic understanding of love is the desire for the union of complementarity.

Secondly, we miss in the account we have reviewed the belief on the part of the lover that the well-being of the beloved is a passionate goal. On the aesthetic level, which takes in the romantic tradition, we might have expected the lover to claim that the well-being of the beloved was his or her only concern, that no obstacle could prevent the lover from caring for the needs of the beloved. We might have called this unselfish view of aesthetic love into question, pointing out the self-oriented agenda which always lies behind eros, even when it is manifested as the desire for the union of complementarity. But in fact we find almost no attention at all being directed to this otherwise popular self-understanding of romantic love.

This gap may well be an indication of Kierkegaard's own view of love superimposed on the aesthetic account of love. For he well knew the selfish orientation of aesthetic love, and the notion of a selfless romantic love may have been simply so foreign to his view that he did not wish to distract his reader by exploring its mistaken self-understanding.

NOTES
CHAPTER ONE

(1) James Collins, <u>The Mind of Kierkegaard</u> (Chicago; Henry Regnery Co., 1967), p. 44.

(2) Søren Kierkegaard, <u>Fear and Trembling/Sickness Unto Death</u>, p. 146.

(3) <u>Ibid.</u>, p. 147.

(4) Søren Kierkegaard, <u>The Concept of Dread</u>, trans. with intro. by Walter Lowrie (Princeton: Princeton University Press, 1970), p. 38.

(5) <u>Ibid.</u>, p. 39.

(6) Søren Kierkegaard, <u>Fear and Trembling/Sickness Unto Death</u>, pp. 148, 149.

(7) <u>Ibid.</u>, p. 177.

(8) <u>The Encyclopedia of Philosophy</u>, reprint ed., s.v. "Romanticism," by Crane Brinton.

(9) Søren Kierkegaard, <u>Either/Or I</u>, p. 74.

(10) <u>Ibid.</u>, p. 76.

(11) <u>Ibid.</u>, p. 79.

(12) Ronald Grimsley, <u>Søren Kierkegaard and French Literature</u> (Cardiff: University of Wales Press, 1966), p. 12.

(13) Søren Kierkegaard, <u>Either/Or I</u>, p. 83.

(14) <u>Ibid.</u>, p. 93.

(15) <u>Ibid.</u>, p. 97.

(16) Christian Dietrich Grabbe, <u>Don Juan und Faust</u> (Leipzig: G. Wigard, 1909).

(17) Søren Kierkegaard, <u>Either/Or I</u>, p. 204.

(18) <u>Ibid.</u>, p. 205.

(19) <u>Ibid.</u>, p. 363.

(20) <u>Ibid.</u>, p. 364.

(21) <u>Ibid.</u>, p. 303.

(22) Ibid., p. 376.

(23) Søren Kierkegaard, Repetition: An Essay in Experimental Psychology (New York: Harper and Row, 1964), p. 36.

(24) Ibid., p. 39.

(25) Ibid.

(26) Ibid., p. 117.

(27) Ibid., p. 136.

(28) Søren Kierkegaard, Fear and Trembling/Sickness Unto Death, p. 104.

(29) Ibid., pp. 104-105.

(30) Søren Kierkegaard, Either/Or I, p. 184.

(31) Ibid., p. 178.

(32) Ibid.

(33) Ibid., p. 189.

(34) Ibid., p. 202.

(35) Ibid., p. 203.

(36) Ibid., p. 252.

(37) Ibid.

(38) Ibid., p. 376.

(39) Ibid., pp. 363, 364.

Chapter II
Ethical Love
Aesthetically Considered

The great enemy of life, the root of all evil aesthetically understood, is boredom, the sense of being trapped and unfree to seek out new and refreshing experiences. The defense proposed against boredom is "rotation," preliminarily defined as "a change of field," (1) but distinguished from a farmer's pattern of intentional crop rotation by its arbitrariness.

> The whole secret lies in arbitrariness. People usually think it easy to be arbitrary, but it requires much study to succeed in being arbitrary so as not to lose oneself in it, but so as to derive satisfaction from it. One does not enjoy the immediate but something quite different which he arbitrarily imports into it. You go to see the middle of a play, you read the third part of a book. By this means you insure yourself a very different kind of enjoyment from that which the author has been so kind as to plan for you. You enjoy something entirely accidental; you consider the whole of existence from this standpoint. . . . (2)

To achieve rotation and avoid boredom requires forgetfulness and the avoidance of any experience that would be so significant as to compel memory. In terms of human relations this means first, the avoidance of friendship, characterized as "mutual assistance in word and deed." (3) "A" calls this relationship into question since "it is impossible for one human being to be anything to another human being except in his way." (4)

The other compelling experience to be avoided is marriage, for, according to the aesthete, the promise to love each other eternally is meaningless and is the ultimate threat of imprisonment in bordom. The only hope is to maintain the possibility of arbitrary termination of love relationships:

> But because a man does not marry, it does not follow that his life need be wholly deprived of the erotic element. And the erotic ought also to have infinitude; but poetic infinitude, which can just as well be limited to an hour as to a month. When two beings fall in love with one another and begin to suspect that they were made for each other, it is time to have the courage to break it off. . . . (5)

Ethical love appears boring to the self-conscious aesthete because it is characterized by duty and duration, whereas love on the aesthetic level

29

seems free only so long as it is characterized by arbitrary self-concern and brevity.

This mocking strategy for dealing with the ethical can be seen also in "The Banquet," where a group of aesthetes have gathered in strict aesthetic protocol. The group agrees to a round of speeches on love and the relationship between men and women, with the provision that all is to be said and understood "in vino," i.e., under the influence of wine. The talk quickly turns to a mocking of love and women.

An unnamed young man, who describes himself in terms reminiscent of the page in Figaro as presented above by "A," starts off the speeches by claiming that love is comic from the perspective of the uninitiated. Constantine Constantious argues that woman is jest; Victor Eremita maintains that woman is a negative; the ladies' tailor discusses how he sees the weakness of women in their desire to be fashionable. Johannes the Seducer proclaims that he loves women just as they are: a deception of the gods to control men and lure them into captivity through marriage. It is the role of the erotic to dine on this bait of the gods and never be caught. (6)

Yet the banquet ends on a less militant note. As they adjourn, they come across Judge William and his wife drinking tea in their garden at the break of day. After all of the discussion of the comic, jest, and deception uttered in vino, William Afham, the observer/author of this writing, asks whether the wife was playing or serious at serving the tea:

> The way the wife busied herself with the tea-table did seem to indicate the assurance acquired by long practice, and yet she showed an almost childish eagerness in this occupation, as if she were a recently wedded woman in that intermediate state where she does not yet know definitely whether marriage is play or earnest, whether being a housewife is a business or a game or a pastime. (7)

The very quiet and unromantic scene of married life becomes strangely appealing to the weary chronicler of the previous night's events.

> In case someone is not ordinarily a tea-lover, he ought to have sat in the Judge's place, for at that moment this drink seemed to me most inviting, and only the inviting look of the kind lady herself seemed more inviting. (8)

If the aesthetes of the banquet had spoken out of wine in the night, the married couple spoke out of tea in the morning, but they too were discussing jest: the jest of Danish law which permits a husband to beat his wife but nullifies itself by failing to spell out the occasions where this may be done. The contentment of the couple playfully at tea is strangely acceptable to the one who is recollecting the aesthetic experience.

Another aesthetic view of ethical love is found in Fear and Trembling, where ethical love is compared to love and faith on the religious level. Johannes de silentio, in struggling with the story of Abraham's sacrifice of Isaac, states that he can understand the dynamic of love in the figure of the tragic hero, even if the ethical level on which this figure lives is not the level of Johannes. The tragic hero is one who gives up the one he or she loves because of duty to a universal value. Agamemnon, for example, sacrifices his daughter so that the gods will give wind to the ships. In contrast to the ridicule of "A" for love on the ethical level, Johannes de silentio views it with respect and even sympathy. Yet he knows that it is different from the love of Abraham, at which he can only marvel. For Abraham not only could give up the beloved son, but also could believe that he would get him back again. Johannes is reduced to silence by the distinction between love on the ethical and religious levels. For it becomes impossible to discern externally the difference between the disregard of the ethical by the aesthete and the disregard of the ethical by Abraham. To the aesthete religious love must appear the same as aesthetic love. Yet Johannes knows that somehow there is a diffenece. (9)

In summary, ethical love appears as selfless to the aesthete. It may be a selfless love of family or even a selfless surrender of the love of family to the duty of a higher value. The aesthete vaguely perceives that ethical love would call the self-oriented agenda of aesthetic love into question, and wants to put as much distance as possible between itself and the ethical.

NOTES
CHAPTER TWO

(1) Søren Kierkegaard, Either/Or I, p. 287.

(2) Ibid., p. 295.

(3) Ibid., p. 291.

(4) Ibid.

(5) Ibid., p. 294.

(6) Søren Kierkegaard, Stages on Life's Way, trans. Walter Lowrie, intro. Paul Sponheim (New York: Schocken Books, 1967), pp. 46-88.

(7) Ibid., p. 90.

(8) Ibid., p. 91.

(9) Søren Kierkegaard, Fear and Trembling/Sickness Unto Death.

31

Chapter III
Ethical Love
Ethically Considered

The Ethical Level

When Kierkegaard described the ethical level of existence, he closely aligned it with the ethics of Immanuel Kant, particularly in Kant's injunction that the maxim under which one acts should be universally applicable. It is the notion that the ethical life realizes the universal that he focused upon in his various treatments of this level.

In contrast to the variety of accounts on the aesthetic level, the account of the ethical level is surprisingly unified. Its principal spokesperson is Judge William the Assessor, the married friend of the unnamed aesthete designed "A," giving forth a comfortable account of the conventional wisdom of society on the limits of aesthetic life, punctuated by an occasional profundity.

Ethical life is characterized by choice:

What is it, then, that I distinguish in my either/or? It is good or evil? No, I would only bring you up to the point where the choice between the evil and the good acquires significance for you. Everything hinges upon this. As soon as one can get a man to stand at the crossways in such a position that there is no recourse but to choose, he will choose the right. (1)

It is choice that the aesthetic level avoids, either by remaining immersed in the immediate or by being distracted by the multiplicity of options.

Your choice is an aesthetic choice, but an aesthetic choice is no choice. . . . The aesthetic choice is either entirely immediate and to that extent no choice, or it loses itself in the multifarious. . . . When a man deliberates aesthetically upon a multitude of life's problem, as you did in the foregoing, he does not easily get one either/or, but a whole multiplicity. (2)

Judge Williams is less concerned with the will to choose the right than he is with the "pathos with which one chooses," (3) not so much because he believes that the choice made from deep pathos will necessarily be for the right (though he does indicate such a view), but because he desires to bring his reader, the aesthete, to the point of choosing with deep pathos, which is the passageway to the ethical level.

To speak of choice is also to speak of despair, for "despair itself is a choice," (4) and thus Judge Williams urges "A" to choose despair, holding before him a story of aesthetic love transformed by despair.

> Imagine a young man as talented as you are. Let him love a girl, love her as dearly as himself. Let him ponder in a quiet hour upon what it is he has constructed in his life and upon what she can construct hers. Love they have in common, and yet he will feel that there are differences. She possesses, perhaps the gift of beauty, but this has no importance for him, and after all, it is so fragile; she has, perhaps, the joyful temper of youth, but that joy has no great significance for him, but he possesses the power of the mind and feels the might of it. He desires to love her in truth, and it never occurs to him to attribute this power to her, and her meek soul does not demand it, and yet there is a difference, and he will feel that this must be done away if he is to love her in truth. Then he will let his soul sink into despair. It is not for his own sake he despairs but for hers, and yet it is for his own sake too, for he loves her as dearly as himself. Then will despair devour everything till he finds <u>himself</u> in his eternal validity, but then he has also found her. . . . (5)

In the usage of Kierkegaard and his pseudonyms, it is possible to be in despair, i.e., in a state of romantic melancholy, without despairing, i.e., without choosing despair. But when one despairs, one is already out of despair as a passive melancholy state, for one has chosen "oneself in one's eternal validity." (6)

Love on the Ethical Level

Because the ethical level is characterized by choice, the model for ethical love is marriage. In contrast to the aesthete who constantly "hovers over himself," (7) and is thus poised to change as desire or expediency dictate, marriage begins with its vow of constancy and faithfulness:

> First (aesthetic) love is strong, stronger than the whole world, but the instant doubt occurs to it, it is annihilated, it is like a sleepwalker who with infinite security can walk over the most perilous places, but when one calls his name he plunges down. Marital love is armed; for by the resolution the attention is not directed merely towards environment, but the will is directed towards itself, towards the inward man. (8)

To be married is to realize the universal in one's love, (9) for the ethical tells one that he should marry, though not to whom. Kierkegaard can even go so far as to have a pseudonym inquire whether there are any exceptions to the maxim that all should marry. (10) Married love realizes the universal, not only because of its commitment, but because it, like

34

friendship, is love that is revealed and "it is every man's duty to become revealed." (11)   In contrast to the reticence and hidden agenda of the aesthetic level, ethical love is open. In this regard Judge William retells the story of Roland's squire, who by use of a magic thimble which made him invisible gained access to the chamber of princess Urraca. She was very impressed with his profession of love, but in order to proceed with the love affair, the squire had to reveal himself, risking the disenchantment of the princess if there were too great a difference between her fantastical image of him and his actual appearance. (12)

It is married love that reveals, sets the record straight, and resolves the impediments that would distract aesthetic love. This is further illustrated in the story of the oriental scholar, who was late to his wife's meal. He had discovered a new mark on a text, a mark which completely altered the existing state of the discipline of study. It was only after his wife had blown upon the page and removed the speck of snuff which provided such arcane distraction that the mystery was revealed and the dinner was enjoyed. (13)

Married love is not simply revealed love, but as such, it is also historical. It takes place in the context of time and in continuity with the human family from the very beginning. Thus the marriage vows are taken, not privately, but before the congregation and with reference to the history of the face.

What, then does the wedding ceremony accomplish? It provides a survey of the genesis of the human race, and therewith it grafts the new marriage upon the great body of the race. Thereby it presents the universal, the essentially human, and evokes it in consciousness. (14)

In contrast to the fleeting moments of beauty on the aesthetic level, beauty is seen ethically as the passion of commitment to those to whom one is related. In such a love one's beloved is not desired on the basis of youthful beauty.

Woman as a bride is more beautiful than as a young girl, as a mother she is more beautiful than as a bride, as wife and mother she is a good word spoken in due season, and with the years she becomes more beautiful. . . .. He sees her beauty, for one loves the beautiful, and this is to be understood as identical with this, that loving is seeing the beautiful. (15)

According to Judge William, there is no more passionate commitment than that of a mother to a child. He observes mothers in public. A well-to-do young mother has taken her two-and-a-half-year-old son for a walk. He is asking questions about the things he sees, and she lovingly answers. Finally he demands to be carried. This obviously was not a part of their understanding, or else a nursemaid would have been brought along. Despite the fact that this could be embarrassing for a person of her standing, she picked up the boy and carried him without the slightest hesitation. (16) On another occasion the assessor noticed how in church a young mother handled the impatience and playfulness of her child. Though he moved around in the pew so much that the priest was distracted, the mother divided her attention between prayer and childcare without irritation. (17)

These everyday examples of a mother's love are seen by Judge William to be indications of a love that has continuity even to times of extreme danger and sacrifice.

And how manifold the collisions to which mother love is exposed, and how beautiful the mother is when her self-denying, self-sacrificing love comes through the trials victoriously! (18)

The happiness of married love consists in all of life having importance. Aesthetic love focuses the entire concentration on the beloved; all else is of no interest. But in married love the lover is freed for a concrete and realistic relationship to the world, and can love with a love that has continuity in all areas of living. Thus the judge catalogues how he loves all about his life; his wife and her relationship to their children, his satisfaction at watching the children mature, his work, his country, his mother tongue.

Thus my life has significance for me, so much so that I feel joyful and content with it. With all that, I live at the same time a higher life, and when sometimes it occurs that I inhale and infuse this higher life in the respiration of my earthy and domestic life, I count myself blessed, and art and grace coalesce before me. Thus I love existence because it is beautiful and hope for an existence still more beautiful. (19)

It is not hard to see also why the ethical includes a sense of vocation which is lacking in the aesthetic. This network of love includes the love of one's calling and the way it relates oneself to other selves.

The ethical thesis that every man has a calling is the expression for the fact that there is a rational order of things in which every man, if he will, fills his space in such a way that he expresses at once the university-human and the individual. (20)

The ethical level is not only characterized by love of vocation, of friends, of spouse, of children, in a style of open self-revelation. It also understands itself as love to God.

What is a man without love? But there are many sorts of love: I love a father and a mother differently, likewise my wife, and every distinct sort of love has its distinct expression; but there is also a love by which I love God, and there is only one word in the language which expresses it. . . . it is repentance. (21)

The ethical level as the choice of self, even the choice of oneself in despair, is a choice of repentance, the willingness to be guilty before God.

This is the truest and most absolute expression of love for God. And to relate despair to repentence is to understand it on a new and deeper level. Repentance is the despair of possessing the meaning and ground of one's life within oneself. And to despair in this way is to "choose oneself in one's eternal validity" by relating oneself through the ground of self, God.

In choosing oneself, relating to oneself through God, the ground of self, the individual relates to the universal. "He who lives ethically labors to become the universal man." (22) Thus duty, the realization of the universal, is not an imposition from without but an expression from within. It is freedom.

Love on the ethical level manifests all these characteristics. It is seen in the commitments of friendship and marriage, where the self is revealed rather than hidden as in aesthetic love. It accepts the commandment to love as integral to its nature, and understands love as joyous obligation.

Friendship

Although marriage is the model for ethical love, Judge William does not ignore the love of friendship. In fact, the whole discussion of marriage has as its context the essays written to a younger friend: ". . . you, in spite of all your bizarre qualities, I love as a son, as a brother, as a friend; . . . (23)

Yet Judge Williams characterizes the ethical man as having the duty to be revealed, to be open to a relationship in which the inner-most heart is shared. And he well knows that the mutuality of a true friendship demands such openness. Since the aesthete "A" clings to his reserve, their friendship is only a potential one.

So receive my greeting, accept my friendship; for though I dare not in the strictest sense characterize our relation as friendship, yet I hope that my younger friend will one day become so much older that I may truthfully use this word. (24)

According to the judge, friendship demands a maturity, a steadfastness, that his junior of eight years does not possess, and that is best found in married persons. People who make friendship their basic expression of love early in life often find that is eclipsed by romantic love and the true value of friendship is lost. Likewise those who rebound from romantic love into friendship are missing its true value. But when a married person becomes a friend, these misunderstandings do not occur.

In his love he found the deepest and most complete satisfaction, but precisely because he was thus absolutely set at rest, there now was opened up to him the possibility of a different relationship which in another way might acquire for him a profound and beautiful significance. . . .

But precisely because it was by and with his marriage he learned to see the beauty in having a friend or friends, he has not been for an instant perplexed as to how he ought to regard friendship. . . . (25)

It is marriage then, that sets one free to participate fully in friendship. The love of friendship is in a secondary and dependent relationship to marriage for the judge, and thus he can say of friendship that "the ethical factor in it has not the same degree of validity as it has in marriage." (26) As highly as he values friendship (and the judge can say that it is the duty of every man to be in that open and reciprocal relationship), (27) it does not have the primacy that friendship has, for example, in the writings of Aristotle, where friendship is the model for true love. For Judge William, the model is marriage.

Immediacy on the Ethical Level

It remains for us to consider whether married love still contains the passionate intensity of aesthetic love. Is Judge William's affable contentment not more characteristic of a cozy friendship, after all, than an all-consuming love affair? Has he, in fact, substituted friendship as the model for ethical love including marriage while claiming to do the opposite? These questions are answered when we explore the issue behind them: What is the role of immediacy on the ethical level?

In attempting to deal with these questions we must never lose sight of the judge's agenda. He is attempting to show how marriage could be desirable to the aesthete on aesthetic grounds. His task is:

... to show the aesthetic significance of marriage; and to show how the aesthetic element in it may be held fast in spite of the manifold obstacles of actual life. (28)

Thus his description of marriage must show how those rare, intense, and fleeting experiences of aesthetic love are less beautiful than the everyday, durable experience of married love. All the foregoing will be unconvincing unless the all-consuming immediacy of aesthetic love can in some sense be repeated on the ethical level. In this context Judge William comes to grips with the issue of first love.

We have already seen how "A" appreciates Scribe's spoof on the belief that the first love is the only true love. Although he is aware of the intensity of feeling that first love can evoke, "A" maintains a moderated cynicism toward this unflective passion.

Although first love may be bittersweet on the aesthetic level, Judge William does not look upon it as sad or tragic.

For me this phrase, "the first love," contains no sadness at all, or at all events only a little seasoning of sad sweetness; for me it is a battle cry, and although I have been for several years a married man,

I still have the honor of fighting under the victorious banner of first love. (29)

The judge is set on showing that "First love can co-exist with marriage," that is "can be assumed into a higher concentricity," and that first love becomes historical in marriage while romantic love is unhistorical. (30) But here we note that he is not identifying romantic love and first love, as did "A." Rather he is contrasting them to make the point that first love is best understood on the ethical level: the real first love is marriage. (31) On the aesthetic level, first love collapses in absurdity; on the ethical and religious level it finds itself in marriage.

Harken and be amazed at the harmonious accord of these different spheres. It is the same thing, except that it is expressed aesthetically, religiously, and ethically. One loves but once. To effect a realization of this, marriage joins in. (32)

It is to be noted that Judge William does not draw as sharp a distinction between the ethical and the religious as does Kierkegaard himself. Rather the religious serves as a convenient justification for ethical values. We see this particularly in the judge's defense of first love as an ethical category.

Aesthetic first love is "eternal," i.e., it does not have continuity in time. It is expressed in the brief and beautiful moment. Ethical first love is historical, continues in time in the form of the commitment of marriage. But this would be unsatisfactory to "A." He would be scandalized by the religious aspect of marriage; that he would have to give up the pretense of being the slave of the beloved and be instated as her master, that before the altar she would be considered as a sinner, and that faithfulness would be lifted out of the arena of desire and become obligation. (33)

All of this signifies that a third power is insinuated into the relationship of first love, that the immediacy of aesthetic love is now mediated by God.

We have seen, then, how first love could come into relation with the ethical and the religious without the intervention of a reflection which would alter its nature, since it was merely drawn up into a higher concentricity, always in the sphere of immediacy. In a certain sense a change has been brought about, and it is this which I will now consider as the metamorphosis (so it might be called) of the lovers into bride and bridegroom. When first love is referred to God, this comes to pass for the fact that the lovers thank God for it. (34)

We note here that there is a departure from what we might have expected as a model of the relationship of love and reflection. The model on the aesthetic level indicated that reflection on unhappy love raised the lover from the immediacy of love to the point where either choice and decision are made (and thus the lover enters the ethical level), or choice is avoided (which drives the lover back into the fruitless pursuit of immediacy). We would have expected that on the ethical level immediacy, that intense and all-consuming love, would be put a side in favor of a warm but controlled relationship in which reflection was an integral part in mediating love between the lovers. But here the possibility is held out for going from immediacy to immediacy, from the immediacy of aesthetic love to an immediacy on the ethical level by referrence to the religious category of marriage. Thus the continuity of first love is preserved and the judge may claim to champion marriage under its banner.

Although Judge William claims to have "shown" how the immediacy of first love is incorporated into the ethical level, it is questionable that he has succeeded. If the price of admission to the ethical level is the conscious relating to the self by choice, even to the point of choosing despair, it is hard to see how this can be "without the intervention of reflection." It would appear that he has introduced the consideration of marriage as a religious category in order to explain how this is possible, yet the explanation needs to be explained. How does the religious account for the continuity of immediacy of first love into the ethical level, or, for that matter, how does it explain immediacy on the ethical level at all?

Several years later Judge William takes another turn at considering the immediacy of first love and its relationship to marriage. In "Various Observations about Marriage in Reply to Objections" he states that, in contrast to the immediacy of aesthetic love, married love is mediated in reflection.

> The enthusiasm of the poet is enlisted by immediacy, the poet is great by reason of his faith in immediacy and its power to prevail. The married man has permitted himself to entertain a doubt, an innocent, a well meant, a noble, a lovable doubt; . . . (35)

This "doubt," this questioning of love, is not fatal to ethical love as to aesthetic love, for ethical love continues in time through decision and choice. The obligation and commitment of love is a positive response to the mediation that requires: "Thou shalt love." This response is called "resolution." Judge William has referred to "resolution" in previous works, but here he gives it more of a specific definition. Resolution is the culminaton of reflection in decision and action. For reflection can continue ad infinitum unless it is brought to a close by decision. When decision occurs, however, this does not mean that reflection has stopped in the sense that all self-conscious thought has ceased, but that the question has been resolved.

In the category of resolution we see Judge William again turning to the religious to understand the relationship of love and reflection in marriage;

> Thus marriage is the beauteous mid-point and center of human existence, giving a reflection as deep as the thing is high which is disclosed by it: a revelation which in cryptic form discloses the heavenly. (36)

In married love the lovers understand that they receive each other from the hand of God. Love penetrates the whole of life and immediacy is made "taut by resolution." (37)

Abandoning the earlier language of "higher concentricity," the judge takes up the image of a "later" immediacy:

... love is itself a later immediacy which enters upon the scene at the time which the will ought to be sufficiently developed to form a resolution as decisive as love understood as immediacy is decisive. So understand, marriage is the deepest, highest, and most beautiful expression of love. Love is the gift of the Deity, but in the resolution of marriage the lover makes himself worthy to receive it. (38)

Thus the later immediacy is a gift of God, a miracle, which bridges that discontinuity between aesthetic and ethical love which the judge now acknowledges.

But again he poses the question, this time in its most incisive expression:

So then I pause here at the decisive point: there must be a resolution superadded to love. But a resolution presupposes a reflection, but reflection is the destroying angel of immediacy. (39)

How, then, in marriage can reflection be concluded and immediacy restored? It is by the gift of faith and the power of God.

On the other hand, reflection is brought to a conclusion in faith, which is precisely anticipation of the ideal infinity in the form of re- solution. Thus the resolution is a new immediacy, attained through the ideally inexhaustible reflection, a new immediacy which corresponds precisely to the immediacy of love. The resolution is a religious life- view constructed upon ethical postulates, which is to prepare the path of love and secure it against every outward and inward danger. (40)

Thus the resolution is in faith, and the later immediacy has its foundation in God, specifically in the belief that married lovers have each other as a gift of God. Thus God replaces reflection as the mediating cate- gory of love on the ethical level: the new immediacy is actually mediation by God:

The immediacy of love recognizes only one other immediacy as of equally noble birth, that is the immediacy of religion; love is too maidenly to recognize any part as privy to it except God. (41)

Judge William has clarified his position with an explicit connection between love and faith. Both are miraculous gifts of God. Both are imme- diate relationships, bringing to a resolution the process of reflection, cul- minating in passionate trust and commitment. Love is a kind of faith, as faith is a kind of love. Second immediacy is possible only through faith in God; in fact, second immediacy is faith in God.

41

The judge has thus extricated himself from the difficulties of his previous model for relating love and reflection in marriage by an appeal to miracle. Although the construct holds together, the ease with which the religious level is brought into proximity reminds us of the earlier difficulties with the continuity between the aesthetic and the ethical levels. Some subtleties of this problem have yet to be explored.

The Possibility of Benevolence

It is more difficult on the ethical level than on the aesthetic to see precisely how the categories of Hazo mesh with the views of love. On the aesthetic level love is acquisitive desire. Strained to the utmost, the aesthetic lover may reach the level of mixed acquisitive desire, where he or she moves beyond the self-oriented gratification of love to a concern for the well-being of the beloved. There is no question of raising the concern of the beloved to primacy as in the case of benevolent love.

Judge William's account of ethical love offers us a less clear picture. At the very least, there is enough concern for the beloved to warrant the category of mixed acquisitive desire. But does the wellbeing of the beloved assume more priority than that of the lover? If so, then ethical love reaches the level of at least self-interested benevolence. And if ethical love comes to be concerned only with the well-being of the beloved, then the level of disinterested benevolence has been reached.

It is doubtful that Judge Wiliam intended to make this distinction, except in the one instance which we shall discuss below. His agenda was to make ethical love appealing to the aesthete and thus he concentrated on getting the attention of a person whose love was self-centered. To argue for the "aesthetic validity of marriage" is to attempt to justify ethical love on the grounds of aesthetic, self-oriented love.

I am going to argue, however, even if the judge did not intend a clear distinction between acquisitive desire and benevolence, that his account of love on the ethical level falls mostly within the realm of benevolence.

Judge William gives at least one clear example of what, for him, is disinterested benevolence. To him the love of a mother for a child is the epitome of self-sacrificing love, devoid of all self-interest. We may want to question whether distinterested benevolence is possible and whether there might be some subtle return of good to the mother, even when sacrificing herself for the child. But at least in the judge's view, there is one example of clear distinterested benevolence.

But the next thing to notice is that, for Judge William, there is a continuity of love on the ethical stage. Once the person has chosen himself or herself despairing that he or she could be the ground of the existence of the self, and once love is committed in marriage as a response to divine command, love flows freely throughout the whole of life. When the judge catalogues above all that he loves, wife, children, vocation, native tongue, country, and friends, he does so out of the bounty of his first love--the intense and immediate love of wife which has never slackened. So the love of parent for child is an overflow of the love between husband and wife. The example of disinterested benevolence above is grounded in marriage and is continuous with it.

Married love must, of course, include self-interest as well. Judge William would be quite willing to admit to this; he testifies long and loud about the benefits of marriage. But it opens out to the possibility of disinterested benevolence, for its focus is on the good for the beloved.

It is not possible categorially to assert that the judge would bar mixed acquisitive desire from the ethical level. In his effort to meet the aesthete on his own ground by showing "the aesthetic validity of marriage," he has used love as the inviting bridge across the qualitative gap getween the aesthetic and the ethical levels. Thus it was not a part of his agenda to sharpen the qualitative distinctions between the entire acquisitive nature of aesthetic love and the generally benevolent nature of love on the ethical level.

But Judge William does make the point that there is a qualitative difference in the self on the two levels. On the aesthetic level the self attempts to be its own ground and will not admit that it has a dialectical nature. It never despairs of finding its own source of meaning, even though it is in despair of finding its true meaning. Such a self is not free to love the other for the other's good. The other is a distraction to keep the self from dealing with itself, i.e., with its dialectical nature. Although the aesthetic lover may say that the beloved is so central and important as to be the whole world for the lover, the total focus of his or her existence, it is not a fully developed self who loves. Rather it is a self who is using the relationship with the beloved to escape the necessity of relating to itself. Thus the motive for aesthetic love will always contain an agenda that is grounded in the despairing self.

In contrast, the self on the ethical level has chosen itself, even in despair. The self is related to itself. Therefore the beloved is not, cannot be, a distraction used by the self to avoid dealing with its dialectical nature. Rather on the ethical level the self is free for the first time to relate to the beloved without a self-oriented agenda. The ethical self is freed for benevolent love.

Again, the distinctions which we are attempting to make are not given in the Danish terms but only in the context. Judge Williams writes of the liberating aspect of love in marriage: "for I have liberated her, also, when I elsker with the youthful enthusiasm for first Kjerligheds." We may, however, identify ethical love with agape as seen in the writings of Paul. Judge William understands married love as a gift of God which brings benevolence toward the other. He also, in contrast to the Johannine understanding, maintains a distinction between the love of others and the love of God, which he defines as repentance. This also is similar of Paul, who seldom used <u>agape</u> for our response to God, since <u>agape</u> was seen as spontaneous and unmotivated love.

Judge William does not, however, explore in any depth the source of ethical <u>agape</u>. He is content to accept God's gift and rejoice in it. A further understanding of <u>agape</u> must take place on yet a higher level.

NOTES
CHAPTER THREE

(1) Søren Kierkegaard, <u>Either/Or I</u>, trans. Walter Lowrie (Garden City, New York: Doubleday and Company, 1959), p. 172.

(2) <u>Ibid</u>., pp. 170, 171.

(3) <u>Ibid</u>., p. 171.

(4) <u>Ibid</u>., p. 215.

(5) <u>Ibid</u>., p. 213.

(6) <u>Ibid</u>., p. 217.

(7) <u>Ibid</u>., p. 11.

(8) <u>Ibid</u>., p. 96.

(9) <u>Ibid</u>., p. 306.

(10) Søren Kierkegaard, <u>Stages on Life's Way</u>, pp. 165-178.

(11) Søren Kierkegaard, <u>Either/Or I</u>, p. 327.

(12) <u>Ibid</u>., pp. 205, 206.

(13) <u>Ibid</u>., pp. 313, 314.

(14) <u>Ibid</u>., p. 91.

(15) Søren Kierkegaard, <u>Stages on Life's Way</u>, p. 141.

(16) <u>Ibid</u>., p. 137.

(17) <u>Ibid</u>., p. 139.

(18) <u>Ibid</u>., p. 137.

(19) Søren Kierkegaard, <u>Either/Or I</u>, p. 329.

(20) <u>Ibid</u>., p. 297.

(19) Søren Kierkegaard, Either/Or I, p. 329.

(20) Ibid., p. 297.

(21) Ibid., p. 220.

(22) Ibid., p. 260.

(23) Ibid., p. 6.

(24) Ibid., p. 337.

(25) Ibid., p. 323.

(26) Ibid., p. 321.

(27) Ibid., p. 327.

(28) Ibid., p. 8.

(29) Ibid., p. 38.

(30) Ibid., p. 47.

(31) Ibid., p. 60.

(32) Ibid., pp. 60, 61.

(33) Ibid., pp. 55, 56.

(34) Ibid., p. 58.

(35) Søren Kierkegaard, Stages on Life's Way, p. 110.

(36) Ibid., pp. 120, 121.

(37) Ibid., p. 146.

(38) Ibid., p. 147.

(39) Ibid., p. 155.

(40) Ibid., p. 159.

(41) Ibid.

Chapter IV
Aesthetic Love
Ethically Considered

In "Equilibrium Between the Aesthetic and the Ethical in the Composition of Personality," Judge William outlines the deficiencies of the aesthetic self-analysis:

> Moreover, I have no doubt that in many ways I shall be able to enlighten you about what it is to live aesthetically. Although I would send to you as the most reliable guide any man who wished to live aesthetically, I would not send him to you if, in a higher sense, he wished to perceive what it is to live aesthetically, for about that you could not enlighten him, precisely because you are enmeshed; only he can do that who stands on a higher level and lives ethically. ... The reason why the man who lives aesthetically can in a higher sense explain nothing, is that he constantly lives in the moment, yet all the time is conscious only in terms of a certain bounds. (1)

It is only at the boundary of the aesthetic level that love has sufficient self-consciousness to reflect upon itself.

The basic characteristic of the aesthetic life, according to Judge William, is its lack of true choice.

> Think of the captain on his ship at the instant when it has to come about. He will perhaps be able to say, "I can either do this or that;" but in case he is not a pretty poor navigator, he will be aware at the same time that the ship is all the while making its usual headway, and that therefore it is only an instant when it is indifferent whether he does this or that. So it is with a man. If he forgets to take account of the headway, there comes at last an instant when there is no longer any question of an either/or, not because he has chosen but because he has neglected to choose, which is equivalent to saying, because others have chosen for him, because he has lost his self. (2)

Not to choose is to lose oneself and, to Judge William the assessor, whose whole life is characterized by decision, the aesthetic life is thus the life of a lost self. Within the aesthetic level the judge sees great diversity, from complete stupidity to great cleverness, but the essential and common element is that the spirit never emerges. It remains hidden by distractions such as talent and physical beauty.

In some rare cases these are quite lasting, as in the assessor's story of the handsome count and countess he met while a child. From the time of their youth even into old age, the couple was acutely aware of its attractiveness, and remained happy in this unusually lasting state. (3) But the judge notes that those whose lives are defined by the pursuit of enjoyment or beauty have the condition for happiness outside of themselves, and must always live with the possibility that events over which they have no control will deprive them of the condition of their happiness.

> In this connection I would also speak of a certain kind of love. If I picture to myself a young girl heart and soul in love, whose eye knew no pleasure but in seeing her lover, whose soul had no thought but him, whose heart had no desire but to belong to him, for whom nothing in heaven or on earth had any significance except him, then here we have again an aesthetic view of life, where the condition is located outside the individual. You, of course, regard it as foolish to be in love in this fashion, you think of it as something which occurs only in romances. (4)

Yet this is not entirely the case, for "A" has revealed his romanticism with a story he once told at Judge William's house, while trying to impress two young Swedish girls. "A" claims to have faith, because he believes that in a dark mysterious forest there lives all alone a nymph of incredible beauty.

> ". . . I believe that I should be happy, the only man deserving to be so called, if I could catch her and possess her; I believe that in my soul there is a longing to search the whole world, I believe that I should be happy if that longing were satisfied; I believe that after all there is some meaning in the world if only I could find it--do not say, then, that I am not strong in faith and fervent in spirit. (5)

Although the whole statement is mock-serious, at least in the judge's understanding, it does illustrate his point. On the aesthetic level the condition of satisfaction is always outside oneself. In the case of "A," the condition for satisfaction lies in locating the nymph in the forest.

As Judge Williams points out, this condition is a despairing one, for one's happiness is dependent upon the "accidental," i.e., on what is outside one's power. He refers us again to the young girl.

> Observe that it is for this reason I said and still say that the young girl was equally in despair whether she got the loved one or not, for in fact it was an accidental circumstance if the man she loved was so upright that he would help her out of her heart's delusion. . . . (6)

This despair, however, is passive despair; it is being in despair without despairing, i.e., without choosing to despair, for when one actively despairs, the process has begun for one's happiness to be more than accidental.

As the aesthetic lover moves from the deepest levels of immediacy toward self-consciousness and fails to find satisfaction in the pleasures and conquests he or she projects, love becomes melancholy, a retreat, a turning back of the spirit upon itself in an indecisive and unconscious manner.

What, then, is melancholy? It is hysteria of the spirit. There comes a moment in a man's life when his immediacy is, as it were, ripened and the spirit demands a higher form in which it will apprehend itself as a spirit. Man, so long as he is immediate spirit, coheres with the whole earthly life, and now the spirit would collect itself, as it were, out of this dispersion and become in itself transformed, the personality would be conscious of itself in its eternal validity. If this does not come to pass, if the movement is checked, if it is forced back, melancholy ensues. (7)

An example of this is to be seen in the Roman emperor Nero, who had in his power all of the conditions to satisfy his desires, but who remained a child on the throne. His pleasures became destructive; his love atrophied to lust. (8)

This general emptiness of aesthetic melancholy is also reflected in attitudes toward vocation. In a recasting of the story of the oriental scholar and the speck of snuff (which we reviewed in the previous section), Judge William had the scholar unmarried. After discovering the exciting vocalization which called the present state of scholarship in this field into question, the scholar visits his lady love in a romantic tryst. He makes no mention of his discovery, for she alone must be the focus of his passion.

But when at dawn he left her, when he had thrown her the last kiss and then sat in his carriage, his brow was darkened. He arrived home, the shutters were closed in his study, the lamps lit, he would not be undressed but sat and stared at the dot he could not explain. He had indeed a girl whom he loved, yea, perhaps adored, but he visited her only when his soul was rich and strong, but he had no helpmeet who came in and called him at midday, no wife who could blow the dot away. (9)

The emptiness is to be seen in the fact that romantic love and the love of life which animates vocation are in conflict, not in harmony as in the first telling of the story.

Though marriage is the model for ethical love, Judge Williams does note that it is possible to carry out the form of marrying without actually being on the ethical level. In "Various Observations about Marriage in Reply to Objections," he tells the story of the wedding of Aladdin. As he prepares for his wedding, Aladdin's desire is intense: "The only thing that concerns him is 'that beloved and long-desired mystical night.'" (10) But his love is immediate. Although he celebrates the wedding, he does not truly marry, for he lacks "a spirit of resolution which in its intensity and concreation corresponds to what his wish is in boundless extension and abstraction." (11) Though he is married, Aladdin is a seducer, and when the immediacy leaves him, so also does the love.

Though some problems remain with Judge William's account of how the ethical level fulfills the deepest goals of aesthetic love, his analysis of the emptiness of aesthetic love is well presented. The arbitrary freedom which aesthetic love celebrates is really unfree decision. The fascination with the beloved turns out to be a fascination with self. The immediacy of aesthetic love is vulnerable. Instead of using the moment of reflective self-consciousness to renew itself, aesthetic love must flee from reflection. In the eyes of the judge, aesthetic love constantly awaits redemption on the ethical level.

NOTES
CHAPTER IV

(1) Søren Kierkegaard, Either/Or I, p. 183.

(2) Ibid., p. 168.

(3) Ibid., pp. 185, 186.

(4) Ibid., p. 187.

(5) Ibid., p. 204.

(6) Ibid., p. 198.

(7) Ibid., p. 193.

(8) Ibid., pp. 189-192.

(9) Ibid., p. 315.

(10) Søren Kierkegaard, Stages on Life's Way, p. 109.

(11) Ibid., p. 110.

Chapter V
Religious Love Aesthetically And Ethically Considered

The Aesthetic View of Religious Love

In "Quidam's Diary," included in Stages on Life's Way, Frater Taciturnus relates as a "psychological experiment" the story of a melancholy man who falls in love. Quidam, which means "Someone," saw and fell in love with a woman, recounting his story in a diary with entries which alternate between the day of record and a year previous to the date.

Even in the dawning of his love Quidam asked: "Ought a soldier of the advanced guard to be married? Dare a soldier on the frontier (spiritually understood) take a wife. . . . ?" (1) After meeting his love at a party, and observing her from afar, Quidam asks for her hand, appealing in writing to her father. They are engaged.

But a year later (the even entries in the diary) he writes: "To see her is a terror to me." (2) His melancholy has asserted itself immediately after the engagement.

And are there not as it were two natures striving within me? . . . I thought that I should be released, that I would be transformed, that seeing myself in love and looking upon her in love, I should behold myself saved, so that I might become like her, a free bird, a youthful song of gladness, that we should grow into one. . . . (3)

This melancholy is related to a "religious crisis": Quidam is too reflective to "keep my soul fixed upon the immediacy of love." (4) He remains in this melancholy, reflective, "religious," viewpoint, but the woman does not have in her personality the capacity for this: she lacks "religious postulates," (5) despite efforts on Quidam's part to cultivate the religious in her.

The similarities to Repetition are striking. Not only is the story line of the diary similar to that of the young man in Repetition, but even the structure of the diary entries is a formal expression of repetition, the attempt to secure the continuity between the meaningful experiences of the past, present, and future. Further, as the young man in Repetition waited for a "thunderstorm and repetition," toward the end of Quidam's story, he is driven by a thundershower into his old refuge from which he would spy on his beloved, and while there sees her again.

51

Quidam systematically attempts to appear unfaithful to her so that she will break off the engagement herself, thus protecting her from a plunge into levels of existence (the religious as he understands it) that she is constitutionally unable to grasp. She half-heartedly breaks off the engagement, but continues to care for him, even to the point of leaving a pleading letter in his room while he is out. He ponders:

> Am I guilty? Yes. How? By the fact that I began what I could not carry to completion. How is it thou dost understand it now? I understand now why it was impossible for me. What then is thy guilt? That I did not understand it earlier. (6)

Finally the relationship is ended, and Quidam continues to suffer the pain of longing for the one he has rejected.

Quidam understands himself to be one living and acting on the religious level of life. "So I have chosen the religious. This lies closest to me, I have put my trust in this." (7) Yet the concept of the religious per se hardly comes through at all, except in Quidam's identification of the religious with his sense of reserve and melancholy. We should not be surprised, then, to find at the end of the diary that the whole thing was a psychological experiment by Frater Taciturnus. The brother admits that he himself is not religious:

> Religious seriousness is, like religion itself, the higher passion which issues from the unity of the comic and the tragic. This I know precisely for the reason that I myself am not religious and have reached this standpoint (that of the unity of the two) without leaping over any preliminary state and without finding the religious in myself. (8)

Also the "someone" of his psychological experiment is actually "a demonic figure in the direction of the religious. . . . " (9) Despite the fact that Quidam understands himself as religious, his creator does not. Rather we are shown how a religious self-understanding can remain within the aesthetic level. Along this line Mackey argues that the figure of Quidam is really an extension of Frater Taciturnus, who cannot make the leap into the religious:

> At last the meaningful non-name Quidam (Someone) stands simply for man, faced with the possibilty and the need of religion but suspended in indecision at the moment of God's approach. The quiet brother finally defined himself as a Sophist who sees the religious and forbears to enact it. . . . (10)

Yet it is important to note that in these multiple layers of authorship, a significant issue is being explored. Kierkegaard is the author of Frater Tacituernus, who as the author of "Quidam's Diary" is recounting events closely resembling Kierkegaard's own life. The giving up of the beloved and the sense of guilt will be seen in a later section to be an account of religiousness A. Yet, since it is the account of Frater Taciturnus, its perspective is from the aesthetic level. Thus what we are given here is an aesthetic perspective on Kierkegaard's love, as if he were only on the level of religiousness A. The similarity with the young man in <u>Repetition</u> also comes clear: Kierkegaard has already portrayed himself as an aesthetic figure and now uses the same story elements to portray himself as a figure on the level of religiousness A. The indirectness of the communication invites us, as it certainly must have invited Kierkegaard's beloved Regina, to re-think what love would look like on each of these levels.

Religious love is difficult also for Johannes de silentio, who explores the distinction between the ethical level and the religious level, though professing that he does not even have the capacity for the ethical level. Johannes states that he can understand the renunciation of one's love on the ethical level, but the double movement of faith in the case of Abraham is beyond him.

As Johannes recounts the Abraham story of the sacrifice of Isaac, he is at pains to make clear that Abraham truly believed that God required the sacrifice of Isaac, and that he continued to believe that the son whom he was about to kill would be the descendant through whom the earth will be blessed. To make this clear he traces scenarios which subtly alter the story and thus qualify the absurdity of Abraham's belief. These show Abraham in despair, renouncing his trust in God's promise for Isaac, reluctantly willing to sacrifice his son, but not capable of a "double movement" of true faith.

According to the parlance of Johannes de silentio, the one who is able to give up what he or she loves because of the call of higher duty is called a "knight of infinite resignation." Thus Antigone gives up the hope for a life of love with her fiancee as she takes up her forbidden duty to bury her rebel brother. Thus Socrates drinks the cup of hemlock in service to the universal duty to obey the law, even when he regards himself as innocent, and even though he has the opportunity to escape.

If Abraham had simply been one of these, a knight of infinite resignation living on the level of the ethical, he would have been guilty of treason against the family. He should have regarded the call to sacrifice Isaac as a temptation to evil and, as the protector of the family, he should have resisted this call. As a member of the family, he was responsible to communicate with Sarah with the matter.

As Johannes presents him, Abraham is moving at a level where the ethical is suspended by absolute duty toward God. He has done more than resign his love for Isaac in favor of obedience to God. Though it is absurd, he also believes that Isaac will still be the child of promise.

> Here the double movement in Abraham's soul is evident, as it was described in the foregoing discussion. If Abraham had merely renounced his claim to Isaac and had done no more, he would in this last word be saying an untruth, for he knows that God demands Isaac as a sacrifice, and he knows that he himself at that instant precisely is ready to sacrifice him. We see then that after making this movement he made every instant the next movement, the movement of faith by virtue of the absurd. (11)

This second movement, by which Abraham resigns his hope for his son, is incomprehensible to Johannes and unrecognizable from the outside. While the knight of infinite resignation is easily recognizable, the knight of faith can be confused with that which is his opposite--the philistine.

For both Abraham and Quidam, the object of their love (a son, a financee) was suitable on the ethical level. Descriptions of the deep care for the good of the beloved place this love at least on the level of self-interested benevolence, if not indeed on the level of disinterested benevolence. It is when these loves encounter the demands of faith that differences begin to emerge.

Both Frater Taciturnus and Johannes de silentio perceive that these loves, when seen on a religious level, can come into conflict with the absolute demands of God. Although these loves remain powerful on the religious level, they must be resigned in favor of duty to the call of God. But as the quiet brother and John of silence have expressed the conflict, it is not a conflict between two loves. It is not a case of loving God more than loving the fiancee or son. It is rather that the demand of God has priority even over the benevolent love of the ethical level. The response to this conflict, once perceived on the religious level, is faith, that happy and highest passion (12) which, like love, involves the whole of existence. In this response Quidam and Abraham are quite different: Quidam resigns his love in duty to his perception of God, as does Abraham. But only Abraham can make the second movement, believing with passionate intensity and despite the paradox that his beloved son will be restored to him. To use Constantine's term, he believes that "repetition" is possible.

Along the same lines, there is a contrast in self-consciousness between the two writings. Frater Taciturnus, in reviewing "Quidam's Diary" which he admits to writing, places himself above his character in understanding what the religious level means. From his vantage point, Quidam is seen as "a demonic figure in the direction of the religious. . . . (13) Johannes de silentio, on the other hand, admits that Abraham is beyond him: "Abraham I cannot understand. . . . (14)

This admission shows the contrast in direction of the two scholars. One has reached the boundary of the ethical, perceived the religious beyond, and turns back into the aesthetic. For him, human love is negated by the demand of God. The other has reached the boundary of the ethical, perceived the religious beyond, and is still straining in that direction, though not yet crossing the aesthetic boundary to another level. He sees that faith may make possible what is impossible for ethical love. The one is simply quiet, the other is silent: the impact of faith upon love has made them so.

The Ethical View of Religious Love

For the most part Judge William does not acknowledge any discontinuity between the ethical and the religious. For him they blend comfortably into each other. We have already seen how he correlates repentence with the ethical love of God, and how the immediacy of married love is mediated by God. However, he does acknowledge an instance which is discontinuous with the ethical. And that is the case of the mystic.

The Christian mystic, at a far deeper level than even the Greek contemplative, has chosen himself, which becomes in absolute freedom the choosing of God also. This choosing is an "inner action":

> The whole world is a dead world for the mystic, he has fallen in love with God. The development of his life is then the unfolding of this love. As there are instances of lovers who have a certain resemblance to one another, also in their outward appearance, their looks, the shape of the face, so too the mystic is absorbed in the contemplation of the Deity, whose image is more and more reflected in his loving soul, and thus the mystic renews and revives the lost divine image in man. (15)

The truest expression of this love is prayer, but not the purposive prayer of the ethical life. Rather, prayer for the mystic aims at fusion.

> As in earthly life the lovers long for the moment when they can breathe out their love for one another and let their souls fuse in a gentle whisper, so the mystic longs for the moment when he in prayer can, as it were, steal in to the presence of God. As the lovers experience the highest degree of bliss in this whispering when really they have nothing to talk about, so for the mystic his soul is all the more blissful, his love a happier one; the less content his prayer has, the more nearly with his sigh he disappears from before his own eyes. (16)

This account of love correlates closely with Hazo's category of love as the desire for the union of similarity.

Judge William finds three faults with the mystic. First, he is "intrusive," claiming a special relationship to God. This is degrading to God and also the mystic. Second, the mystic is soft and weak, needing constant reassurance that his love is genuine and authentic. Third, the mystic ignores the obligation to the human community, setting human relationships against the divine relationship, for loving another as a husband or father is seen as contradictory to loving God.

> He who devotes himself one-sidedly to the mystical life becomes at last so alien to all men that every relationship, even the tenderest, the most heartfelt, becomes indifferent to him. It is not in this sense one is to love God more dearly than father and mother; God is not so self-serving as that, neither is He a poet who wishes to torment men with the most frightful collisions--and hardly could a more frightful thing be conceived than that there might be a collision between love for God and love for the persons for whom love has been planted by Him in our hearts. (17)

Judge William can applaud the mystic's choice of self, for the ethical is a level of choice. His complaint is that the mystic chooses abstractly, and his repentence is abstract. In contrast to that is ethical choice and repentance:

The mystic chooses himself abstractly. One can therefore say that he constantly chooses himself out of the world. But the consequence is that he is unable to choose himself back again into the world. The truly concrete choice is that wherewith at the very same instant I choose myself out of the world I am choosing myself back into the world. (18)

Judge William sees certain parallels between the abstraction of the mystic and the fantastical life of the aesthete. In writing to his aesthetic friend he comments:

Thus you are by no means lacking in the factors which might dispose you, for a time at least, to become a mystic. Here is a field on which the greatest contrasts meet, the purest and most innocent soul with the most culpable, the most talented man and the simplest. (19)

The continuity of love on the ethical level causes the judge to view the mystic's radical love of God as almost an aesthetic love. For the judge the authentic choice of self renders discontinuity as needless, for the love of God and the godly love of others is subsummed in the ethical. In contrast to ethical benevolence, the mystic's desire for God is the acquisitive desire for union.

NOTES
CHAPTER V

(1) Søren Kierkegaard, Stages on Life's Way, p. 188.

(2) Ibid., p. 207.

(3) Ibid., p. 205.

(4) Ibid., p. 210.

(5) Ibid., p. 223.

(6) Ibid., p. 348.

(7) Ibid., p. 211.

(8) Ibid., p. 399.

(9) Ibid., p. 436.

(10) Louis Mackey, <u>Kierkegaard: A Kind of Poet</u> (Philadelphia: University of Philadelphia Press, 1972), p. 254.

(11) Søren Kierkegaard, <u>Fear and Trembling/Sickness Unto Death</u>, p. 128.

(12) <u>Ibid.</u>, p. 131.

(13) Søren Kierkegaard, <u>Stages on Life's Way</u>, p. 436.

(14) Søren Kierkegaard, <u>Fear and Trembling/Sickness Unto Death</u>, p. 48.

(15) Søren Kierkegaard, <u>Either/Or I</u>, p. 247.

(16) <u>Ibid.</u>, pp. 247, 248.

(17) <u>Ibid.</u>, p. 249.

(18) <u>Ibid.</u>, p. 253.

(19) <u>Ibid.</u>, p. 248.

Chapter VI
Religious Love
Religiously Considered

The Religious Level

In exploring how Kierkegaard's figures on the religious level of life view their love, we encounter a problem which was not present on the previous levels. There the figures could be seen as speaking out of their particular level and their views elucidated.

But on the religious level much of what we have to consider is given to us by pseudonyms whose placement is problematic. One of these is Johannes Climacus. The climber shows that the Cartesian program of systematic doubt, particularly in Hegel's version of it with its presuppositionless beginnings, never reaches the level of positive assertion and action. (1) There must be a qualitative leap beyond doubt into decision and action. The endless speculation of philosophy is not prepared to make the leap. In particular, Johannes Climacus shows how this is necessary in the question of faith, for the framework of his writing is the question: How can I, Johannes Climacus, become a Christian?

The problem of placement of Johannes Climacus arises from his attempt to work his way through speculative philosophy to Christianity. Since he sees through the deception that one can speculate one's way into Christianity, he cannot be located on the aesthetic level. Since he sees that more is required than the comfortable acceptance of God's gifts, he is not on the ethical level. But since he is always in the process of becoming a Christian, precisely how can we locate him on the religious level? Thus Kierkegaard says of Johannes Climacus' major work:

> The Concluding Postscript is not an aesthetic work, but neither is it in the strictest sense religious. Hence it is by a pseudonym, though I did add my name as editor--a thing I did not do in the case of any purely aesthetic work. (2)

We will include the writings of Johannes Climacus as religious, because they fit better on this level than on the others, but with the caution that they do not entirely fit here either. The use of the vocabulary and issues of speculative philosophy as a ladder by which to climb into Christianity would be too cumbersome for one ready to take the qualitative leap of faith. Johannes is attempting to climb to Christianity from below. (3) We are further cautioned not to identify precisely the works of a pseydonym with Kierkegaard's own view.

Fortunately we do not have the same difficulty in placing Kierkegaard himself. In The Point of View for My Work as an Author, he repeatedly emphasized that his work was from the very beginning religious, pointing out that the aesthetic works are accompanied by an edifying discourse. (4) His goal as a religious writer has been to reveal the monstrous illusion of a passionless Christianity and to create the possibility of an individual coming to true faith.

But it is through Climacus that the language of speculative philosophy is stretched to give us a picture of the two parts of the religious level of existence. The first of these is called "immanent religions" or "religiousness A," characterized by three expressions of existential pathos.

The first expression is resignation, the maintenance of an absolute relationship to the absolute and a relative relationship to what is relative, for only in this is eternal happiness possible. But this must be done with absolute passion and at every moment:

> When an official of high rank or perhaps the king himself, makes a tour of inspection to ascertain the condition of the public funds, an unfaithful servant may sometimes succeed in having his balances in order for the day of inspection. As soon as the audit is over, he thinks, everything will again slip back into the old ruts. But resignation is not a king on a visit of inspection to examine the accounts of other people; it is in possession of the individual's own consciousness of himself. Nor is resignation a travelling inspector in a passing visit; it takes it upon itself to remain, making every day a day of inspection. . . . (5)

In previous sections of the Postscript, Climacus has explored the relationship between truth and subjectivity, the demands of the authentic self, and the demands of faith. In the passionate inwardness of resignation in the face of the Absolute, all of this comes together, for here all of the relative goods of temporal existence are resigned in favor of the absolute good which is one's eternal happiness.

The second and essential expression of the existential pathos of immanent religion is suffering. Here suffering is not accidental but rather wholly necessary to the religious mode of existence.

> The reality of the suffering thus means its essential persistence as essential to the religious life, while aesthetically viewed, suffering stands in an accidental relation to existence, it may indeed be there but it may also cease, while viewed religiously the cessation of suffering is also the cessation of the religious life. (6)

In suffering immediacy expires and consciousness of oneself as related essentially to God becomes a determinant of life. Here the meaning of passionate inwardness comes to light, for passion is not simply intense feelings: it is suffering. This suffering is not accidental; it is not self-inflicted. It is the realization of helplessness before God.

The third and decisive expression of existential pathos in immanent religion is guilt. In existence each individual is involved in time and is responsible for the use of it. But from the very beginning, the individual is behind in his or her responsibility.

Thus things go backward: the task is presented to the individual in existence, and just as he is ready to cut at once a fine figure. . . and wants to begin, it is discovered that a new beginning is necessary, the beginning upon the immense detour of dying from immediacy, and just when the beginning is about to be made at this point, it is discovered that there, since time has meanwhile been passing, an ill beginning is made, and that the beginning must be made by becoming guilty and from that moment increasing the total capital guilt by a new guilt at a usurious rate of interest. (7)

Guilt is appropriated by the individual through recollection, the grasping of the essential in the past. Thus, on the religious level, we see that one may rightly seek eternal happiness only by acknowledging that one is absolutely guilty before God.

But there is a second level of the religious, called "transcendent religion" or "religiousness B," which is dialectical in a paradoxical way. Religiousness A, which can be paganism, must be present before the individual can move on into religiousness B, which is Christianity.

Religiousness A is the dialectic of inward transformation:

It is the relation to an eternal happiness which is not conditioned by anything but is the dialectic inward appropriation of the relationship, and so is conditioned only by the inwardness of the appropriation and its dialectic. Religiousness B. . . does on the contrary posit conditions, of such a sort that they are not merely deeper dialectical apprehension of inwardness, but are a definite something which defines more closely the eternal happiness. . . . (8)

In religiousness B the awareness of one's passionate inwardness comes up against the absurd. Like the foregoing, this absurdity has three expressions.

In contrast to the person of religiousness A who has resigned the temporal to gain happiness in the eternal, in religiousness B the Christian believes in an eternal happiness given in time itself. Furthermore, this eternal happiness is related to a deity who comes in history, and who can thus be known only in the approximate knowledge of history.

He who with the greatest possible passionateness, in distressful concern for his eternal happiness, is or should be interested in the fact that somebody or another existed, must be interested in the least

61

detail, and yet he cannot attain more than an approximate certainty, and is absolutely in contradiction. (9)

To place one's eternal hope on a historical fact is difficult, but to do so with the realization of the absurdity of the eternal becoming historical is even more difficult.

When religiousness A is surpassed by religiousness B, there are three results: (1) the sense of guilt is sharpened into "sin-consciousness" as a historical and individual reality, (2) the possibility arises that the understanding is offended by a historically based paradox which it cannot comprehend, (3) the sense of sympathy is sharpened for those who cannot or will not attain eternal blessedness by virtue of the paradox.

Johannes Climacus has used the conceptual apparatus of speculative philosophy to climb speculatively toward Christianity and to delineate sharply its boundaries. He has shown how difficult it is to be a Christian. But he, himself, does not claim the title.

The undersigned, Johannes Climacus, who has written this book, does not give himself out to be a Christian; he is completely taken up with the thought how difficult it must be to be a Christian; but still less is he one who, having been a Christian, has ceased to be such by going further. (10)

Climacus describes faith, the act of becoming a Christian, as having one's existence in the dialectic of religiousness B, as becoming contemporaneous with Christ. Those disciples who actually heard and saw Jesus of Nazareth have no advantage on the disciple of the present day. If anything, there was a danger of being distracted by the humility of the God-man while he was here on earth, and thus not see him as the Christ. But neither has the growth of the church in succeeding centuries any effect in drawing us closer to the Christ. Rather the true contemporary of Christ is one who takes the departure of God being in time and history with passionate concern and bases his or her eternal happiness upon that historical event.

The contemporary disciple gets an historical point of departure for his eternal consciousness as well as any later disciple; for he is contemporary with precisely that historical phenomenon which refuses to be reduced to a moment of merely occasional significance, but proposes to interest him in another sense than the merely historical, presenting itself to him as a condition for his eternal happiness. (11)

The passion through which one appropriates this event of God being in time is the happy passion of faith, the capacity for which is a gift of God.

God's Love

Kierkegaard did not dwell at length on the theme of God's love. Yet it is clearly a presupposition to what he writes on human love, for God's love is the hidden source from which all love flows. Kierkegaard gives us two images for this. The first is that of light and its source:

> As God dwells in the light from which streams every beam which lights the world and yet no one can penetrate back by these paths to see God, for the path of light changes to darkness when one turns toward the light: so love dwells in the hidden or is hidden in the inmost depths. (12)

A second and even more powerful image for the source of love is that of a lake and the springs which feed it:

> As a quiet lake is fed deep down by the flow of hidden springs, which no eye sees, so a human being's love is grounded, still more deeply, in God's love. If there were no spring at the bottom, if God were not love, then there would be neither a little lake nor a man's love. As the still waters begin obscurely in the deep spring, so a man's love mysteriously begins in God's love. As the quiet lake invites you to look at it but the mirror of darkness prevents you from seeing through it, so love's mysterious ground in God's love prevents you from seeing its source. (13)

As God's love is hidden, it also hides. In the Journals, Kierkegaard takes up the passage from I Peter 4:7-12 which also appears in an edifying discourse: "Love Shall Cover a Multitude of Sins." But here the love that hides is more explicitly God's love in Christ.

> In Christ everything is revealed—and everything is hidden. Christ's love which indulgently hides the multitude of sins and Christ's love of God, a love which is pleasing to God and under which he hides a multitude of sins. (14)

The love of God in Christ is a forgiving love, as seen in the forgiveness of the woman taken in adultery, whose sins were hidden as Jesus wrote in the sand.

God's love surrounds us not only spatially but also temporarily: it is the first and the last. We are taught to love by imitating divine love.

> We should learn from God what love is. He is indeed the one who first loved us—and thus is our first teacher, who by loving us taught us love so that we could love him. And when. . . you lie down never to get up again, . . . then there still remains one by the deathbed, he who was the first—God. (15)

So then, our whole life is surrounded by God's love.

The theme of forgiveness is again picked up in Kierkegaard's exploration of the Johannine formula that God is love.

No, that God is love means, of course, that he will do everything to help you love him, that is, to be transformed into likeness to him. As I have frequently said, he knows very well how infinitely agonizing this transformation is for a human being; he is willing to suffer with you--yes, out of love he suffers more than you, suffers all the deep sorrow of misunderstanding--but he is not changed. (16)

That is, although the tendency in love is to be transformed into likeness to the beloved, this does not apply to God. Rather God transforms the beloved creatures into likeness to God's loving self. The inducement to love God and become like God is the forgiveness of sins.

Kierkegaard holds in tension two aspects of divine love. The first, which we have already touched upon, is that God through love desires to engender love in his creatures. In exploring this Kierkegaard uses the model of human love for divine.

Now let us see how God proposes, so to speak, to a human being--God, who Christianly may in no way be considered apathetic, for he is such pure passion and pathos that he has only one pathos: to love, to be loved, and out of love wanting to be loved. (17)

But the second aspect of divine love is that it is truly divine, and therein lies the danger that the human response will be unhappy love:

He proposes by saying to a person: I love you, I who am love; be my beloved--the consequence of this will be, and I tell you this at the outset, the consequence will be that you become an unhappy, piteous, wretched man, a byword among men, hated, exiled, persecuted by men, and finally deceived by me. (18)

It is the majestic divinity of God's love which leads to the incarnation. For God's love constantly threatens to overwhelm the fragile synthesis which is the human being, and thus it is by the incarnation that God brings divine love most fully to humanity. An entry in the Journals explores in images of human love the need for the incarnation.

--If a prince loved a poor peasant girl, the task of finding equality would be very difficult. He would not only conceal his royal rank . . . but, if she then desired him to reveal himself as king and to elevate her to his side, he would say that it is unbecoming, and his deep erotic love would be manifested precisely by his concern not to wound her and also not to satisfy her earthly vanity . . . but in truth to love her and become completely equal with her. (19)

A more extended version of this analogy to God's loving incarnation is in Johannes Climacus' Philosophical Fragments. He is discussing the need for a teacher who does more than help one discover the condition for eternal happiness within oneself. Rather there is a need for a savior-teacher who is himself the condition. The motivating factor here must be love: "But if he moves himself, and is not moved by need, what else can move him but love?" (20)

It is only love which can make the incarnation possible.

Moved by love, the God is thus eternally resolved to reveal himself. But as love is the motive so love also must be the end; for it would be a contradiction for the God to have a motive and an end which did not correspond. His love is a love of the learner, and his aim is to win him. For it is only in love that the unequal can be made equal, and it is only in equality or unity that an understanding can be effected, . . . (21)

But then the consideration follows as to the difficulty of this love, as explored in the parable of the king and the maiden: a king loved a humble maiden, but was troubled as to how he might reveal himself to her without overpowering her, for he wanted her to be able truly to love him.

Since we found that the union could not be brought about by an elevation it must be attempted by a descent. . . . In order that the union may be brought about, the God must therefore become the equal of such a one, and so he will appear in the likeness of the humblest. But the humblest is one who must serve others, and the God will therefore appear in the form of a servant. (22)

Thus the reason for the incarnation as the way God would reveal himself and win salvation of creation is to be seen in the dynamics of love. The incarnation is the way love makes love possible.

We cannot emphasize too strongly the radical nature of the incarnation for Kierkegaard and its connection to his notion of divine love. God's transcendence made the incarnation absolutely necessary to bridge the gap with humanity. Yet this act of laying aside the prerogatives of that transcendence in Christ's incarnation and suffering is understandable only when we note the unity of divine power and divine love. Only when we see that divine power is the power to self-limitation and self-effacement do we really come to grips with the extent of that power. Only when we see the king cloaked in the humility of the commoner do we really come to grips with the power and love of the king.

We began our consideration of Kierkegaard's thoughts on divine love by noting that it was not a frequent topic of his. Yet, in spite of this, we have seen that divine love has a central place in his thought. Perhaps the infrequency of Kierkegaard's discussions of divine love was caused by the trivialized manner in which the Danish church understood the God-relationship. To dwell on God's love might make a complacent church even more complacent, whereas Kierkegaard wanted to emphasize the transcendent God whose demands for discipleship were not being taken seriously. Thus, even as Kierkegaard spoke of God's love being hidden, its input for his work is also hidden in his writings.

Human Love for God

The God who is love is the source of our love. We do not love God strictly for himself, for his holiness. Rather we love God through need:

> The man who most deeply recognizes his need of God loves Him most truly. Thou shalt not presume to love God for God's sake; thou shalt eternally understand that thy life's welfare eternally depends upon this, and for this reason thou shalt love him. (23)

Our love for God is therefore not spontaneous and unmotivated (as in Nygren's description of Pauline agape), but is a response motivated by God's love for us, without which we are incomplete. It is, therefore, in Kierkegaard's description, a desire for the union of complementarity, with definite acquisitive overtones. The possibility of renouncing our worldly desires through love of God indicates that the human love of God can reach to the level of mixed acquisitive desire.

Kierkegaard is quite emphatic that the God who is love and who loves us wants us to return that love. This first becomes visible in repentance. Under his Journal heading "What it means to love God," Kierkegaard wrote this fragment: ". . . and you who feel so far removed from your God, what else is your seeking God in repentance but loving God." (24)

But human love moves beyond repentence to a state of blessedness, for "the highest blessedness of a human being is to come to love God properly." (25) This blessedness comes about by God effecting in us a transformation into God's likeness. Although this transformation is painful and demands suffering, God has made it possible by divine suffering.

> No, that God is love means, of course, that he will do everything to help you to love him, that is, to be transformed into likeness to him. As I have frequently said, he knows very well how infinitely agonizing this transformation is for a human being, he is willing to suffer with you--yes, out of love he suffers more than you, suffers all the deep sorrow of misunderstanding--but he is not changed. (26)

The proper response to God's love and suffering, particularly as seen in Christ, is to imitate it. For to love someone is to wish to be like them, to move out of one's own desires into the desires of the beloved, and this is accomplished not just with words but with actions.

> Suppose someone, with the greatest sacrifice, has done me the greatest service, and I now say that I love him--well, observe how I express it and see whether or not I do love Christ who suffered and died for me. Now then, happy that he gained for me the forgiveness of my sins and eternal salvation, I will properly enjoy life but also thank him and again thank him. Hold on there--is that what it means to love Christ? No, it is the very opposite, the most frightful egotism. Or do I now know the way Christ wants me to express my

gratitude--that is, by imitation (Efterfolgelse). (27)

But this love expressed as imitation of Christ will not lead to happiness, as Kierkegaard repeatedly reminds us:

From a Christian point of view, to love God and to be happy and fortunate in this world are not possible. No, the God of Christianity is in contrast to this world; therefore one who loves God Christianly cannot be happy and fortunate in this world. (28)

In addition to the suffering mentioned above, imitation of Christ means also love of neighbor:

Love to God and love to neighbor are like two doors that open simultaneously, so that it is impossible to open one without opening the other, and impossible to shut one without also shutting the other. (29)

In the next section we will explore more fully what the love of neighbor entails.

Finally, with regards to the human love of God, Kierkegaard is emphatic that one cannot love the world and "also" love God, i.e., love both without distinguishing the qualitative difference.

Christianity believes that it is the greatest possible high treason to want to love God also, to enjoy life, be attached to the world, and also love God--even a mere man is not satisfied with also being loved, with being loved also. Dreadful presumption for a miserable nothing like man to want to venture also to love God! (30)

To the objection that we should love and appreciate God's beautiful handiwork, Kierkegaard replies that this clouds the issue, for we participate not only in nature but in the tained processes of human culture. To want to love God "also" betrays an unwillingness to let go of the pleasures of the world and follow the narrow way.

That love to God involves renouncing the world while continuing to love those in the world (the neighbor) holds up to us more precisely what Kierkegaard means by the human love for God. Love to God involves loving the neighbor for God's sake by imitating God's love. Therefore the neighbor is not loved because he or she is pleasing or attractive, but is loved because that is commanded by God. It is impossible to love the world "also", i.e., in addition to loving God, if all our love is a part of our loving God. To love "also," to love for beauty or pleasure, is not to love through loving God. We will explore this further as we look at the Christian love of others.

The Christian Love of Others

Kierkegaard's Works of Love (Kjerlighedens Gjerniger) gives us the most complete insight into his specifically Christian understanding of love for others. We are cautioned at the outset, however, that Christian love is not recognizable as a feeling that we or others might experience (subjectively). Nor is it recognizable by the focus of love (objectively). Christian love is only known by its fruits, works of love, and yet even in its work it is not known essentially. It is hidden.

There are two aspects of the hiddenness of Christian love. As mentioned previously, its source is hidden. God's love, which makes human love possible, is like a deep spring which supplies a lake, or like the source of light which is hidden in the light itself.

Secondly, Christian love is hidden from the unloving by their lack of love, for the works of love are recognizable only by love: "Only he who abides in love can recognize love and in the same way his love is to be known." (31)

In affirming the commandment of Jesus to love your neighbor as yourself, Christianity postulates that everyone loves himself or herself, and demands that only love of God be placed higher than love of self. But what is crucial here is that "the very mark of Christian love and its distinguishing characteristic is this, that it contains the apparent contradiction: to love is duty." (32) But Kierkegaard goes on to contend that only "when it is a duty to love, only then is love eternally secure." (33) Love that arises out of spontaneity is dependent on that spontaneity, which may at any moment change to despair, but love that is rooted in duty is dependent on the eternal.

Erotic love (elskov) and friendship (venskab) are praised by the poet, whose orientation qua poet is essentially within paganism. This love is characterized by spontaneity and intensity:

The point at issue between the poet and Christianity may be stated precisely in this way: erotic love and friendship are preferential and the passion of preference. Christian love is self-renunciation's love and therefore trusts in this shall. (34)

Christianity views erotic love and friendship, even when there is a high degree of benevolence toward the beloved, as essentially self love:

That it is self-love when a faithless person jilts the beloved and leaves the friend in the lurch, paganism saw also--and the poet sees it. But only Christianity sees as self-love the devotion of the lover's surrender to the one and only whereby the beloved is held firmly. Yet how can devotion and boundless abandon be self-love? Indeed, when it is devotion to the other-I, the other-myself. (35)

The neighbor, however, is not the self-chosen other-I, the other self preferred by my self-love. The neighbor is given in the world. The neighbor is anyone and everyone. All men and women are the neighbor. But in order to keep love from becoming an abstraction, Kierkegaard also describes the neighbor as the "next" one, the one I encounter as proximate to me in space and time.

The essential difference between the love of the world and Christian love is a difference of mediation. In the love of the world the relation between the lover and the beloved is mediated by preference. In Christian love, the commandment to love one's neighbor places God in the role of mediator. One can love one's neighbor as oneself because one loves God above all.

In love and friendship preference is the middle term; in love to one's neighbor God is the middle term. Love God above all else and then love your neighbor and in your neighbor every man. Only by loving God above all else can one love his neighbor in the next human being. (36)

This does not mean that one should cease to love the beloved of preferential love, but that when one loves the world, one loves all equally, those beloved of duty and those beloved of preference. Distinctions between the ones who are beloved, however, are not taken away. Rather love mediated by love to God enables one to overcome distinctions. Thus love of neighbor includes also the love of enemy. (37)

Love as a fulfilling of the law demands inwardness, but here again the world's understanding of inwardness is inadequate, for it is preferential:

But divinely understood to love oneself is to love God and truly to love another man is to help him to love God or in loving God. Therefore we see here that inwardness is determined not only by the love-relationship, but by the God-relationship. (38)

Kierkegaard emphasizes throughout that Christian love is not determined by the object, either in present or future forms. Love as duty is not to seek out the lovable object, but to find the given one lovable. (39) It is boundless, unchanging with the changes in the beloved, even as Christ's love was boundless. In contrast to the waxing and waning of erotic love, Christian love abides, for it is grounded in God's love.

In his exposition of I Corinthians 13 Kierkegaard shows how his concept of Christian love closely parallels Hazo's concept of benevolent desire. Love not only hopes all things and believes all things, but seeks not its own, since there is no longer a "one's own." Christian love as benevolence, wherein the primary purpose is to give, is contrasted with acquisitive self-love, which seeks its own by giving in order to receive. Christian love even "gives in such a way that the gift appears to be the receiver's possesion." (40)

Kierkegaard acknowledges that the benevolence of Christian love can have a secondary self-interest, albeit an unconscious one. The stage is set for this when he acknowledges early that self-love is assumed in Christian love: the Christian is to love others as himself or herself. But he goes on to point out how love for the other has a simultaneous inner direction for the lover as well.

> What love does, it is; what it is, it does—at one and the same moment; simultaneously as it goes beyond itself (in an outward direction) it is in itself (in an inward direction), and simultaneously as it is in itself, it thereby goes beyond itself in such a way that this going beyond and this inward turning, this inward turning and this going beyond, are simultaneously one and the same. (41)

Kierkegaard uses as an example of this the saying "love makes for confidence," which means both that love makes the beloved confident and that the lover becomes confident as well. Yet the inner movement of love is not a conscious one, for the lover forgets himself or herself.

> Only love never thinks about the latter, about saving oneself, about acquiring confidence itself; the lover in love thinks only about giving confidence and saving another from death. (42)

The lover becomes so self-forgetful that only God in love remembers the lover. The benevolence of Christian love is thus so characterized by forgetfulness of self that only the unconscious inner movement of love is self-directed and is only the slightest determinant in the direction of self-interested benevolence.

Although Kierkegaard did not use a term such as Hazo's "disinterested benevolence," preferring descriptive language to the generation of terminology at this point, he nevertheless holds out an example of distinterested benevolence as the pinnacle of Christian love for others: remembering in love the dead. For in this love, no possible benefit is offered the lover.

> In order properly to test whether or not love is faithful, one eliminates everything whereby the object could in some way aid him in being faithful. But all this is absent in the relationship to one who is dead, one who is not an <u>actual</u> object. If love still abides, it is most faithful. (43)

Furthermore, if the love one has for those absent in death abides and is unchanged, then it is a model for loving those who are alive but not present, and, by extension, a model for loving those who <u>are</u> present.

Another characteristic of Christian love emphasized by Kierkegaard is that it hides sin, just as we have noted earlier that Christ's love hides a multitude of sins. It hides first of all by not discovering the sin. In contrast to the rest of the world, Christian love maintains a certain child-like innocence:

> The child-likeness, then, is that the lover, as in a game, cannot see with open eyes what takes place right in front of him; the solmnity consists in its being evil which he cannot see. (44)

Secondly, Christian love hides a multitude of sin by silence, for the one who reports a neighbor's faults extends and magnifies the effect of them, while the one who remains silent allows the neighbor's faults to diminish. (45) Third, Christian love hides the multitude of sins by forgiveness. This does not deny the reality of the sin, but takes the forgiven sin away:

> Just as one by faith believes the unseen in the seen, so the lover by forgiveness believes the seen away. Both are faith. Blessed is the man of faith; he believes what he cannot see. Blessed is the lover; he believes away what he nevertheless can see! (46)

Finally, love hides a multitude of sins by preventing their inception. Kierkegaard notes that many things are "occasions" to sin. An occasion is not a cause but a context, an opportunity, the response to which can be sin. But love is the one condition which does not become an occasion to sin. Where true Christian love exists, sin is smothered.

Elsewhere, Kierkegaard dwells on the multitude of the sins which are covered, recalling that "multitude" is used for the innumerable created beings on earth. Christian love is so powerful as to cover even so vast a multitude of sins. (47)

In presenting the idea that Christian love hides sin, Kierkegaard is arguing that this love for others is not only a possible and authentic response to God's love, but that it is an effective one as well. For it is to be seen not as an internal emotion but as an activity: the works of love.

Love on the Religious Level

In referring to God's love and Christian love, Kierkegaard uses the noun kaerlighed (also spelled kjerlighed) wherever possible since it tends to exclude the purely sensual applications of the term for love. However, we are cautioned that kaerlighed is also used for certain kinds of non-Christian love, and therefore can in no way be taken as a special term for love on the religious level. We note also that elske, the only verb form for love, is used both for God's love and for the human response of love.

The obvious beginning for comparison in the Christian tradition is agape, but, as Anders Nygren points out, agape has been used in different ways. In Paul's letters, agape was the spontaneous and self-less love of God for the world and the love in which Christians responded in love to others. Since it was the equality of motivation which characterized agape, Christians were not so much to agape God as to believe God and respond in faith (pistis).

Nygren charts a gradual change in the understanding of agape however, which ends with agape being a general term for God's love and the Christian's love. God is agape; Christians are admonished what to agape and what not to agape. By the time Augustine has entered the picture, the Latin caritas has become the replacement for agape as the term for God's love and the Christian's love. If human love is not to be cupiditas it must be directed

71

toward God and neighbor. In its direction toward God, it is seeking the absolute and changeless good for itself, thus becoming characterized by an acquisitive element.

Kaerlighed in Kierkegaard's writings is used for all but the purely sensual object. It may be applied to God's love for us, our love for God, and even romantic love. Thus it is by no means restricted to the spontaneous and unmotivated love of Pauline agape. It is a little like Augustinian caritas in the sense that pure sensuality is excluded, but unlike caritas in that it may also be directed in unacceptable ways. We also note that the caritas of Augustine is acquisitive, whereas in Kierkegaard kaerlighed may be aquisitive or benevolent.

Although Kierkegaard's use of kaerlighed does not correspond directly with these traditional terms, we can now see more clealry what the issues are for Kierkegaard's concept of Christian love. The source of all love, even that beyond the Christian context, is God's sacrificial benevolence. Even though God pours out love on all and empowers their love on whatever level they live, the goal is to claim them as Christians.

For Kierkegaard God's love is so goal oriented that it is difficult at times to see it as non-acquisitive. Yet it is possible to make the case that finally for Kierkegaard God's love is disinterested benevolence. For he points out that those who respond to God's love become more like God, imitating Christ in his sacrificlal suffering.

We pause to recall here that in Hazo's categories there are two kinds of love as desire for union, and each of them can be either benevolent of acquisitive. The first is the desire for complementarity, where the lover and the beloved each supply a deficiency in the other. One may love benevolently, to supply the need of the other, or acquisitively, to fulfill one's own need. The second kind of love as desire for union is the desire for similarity. The lover and beloved have as the basis for their love the fact that they are like each other in some way. This love is acquisitive if the goal is to benefit the self by relating to the other, or benevolent if the goal is to benefit the other by relating the oneself.

The benevolent desire for complementarity is a useful way to model divine love in Kierkegaard. God seeks to give a good to the beloved by making him or her to be more completely who they are, restoring the relationship for which they were created. Without benefit to God, divine love showers us with gifts, including the gift of eternal happiness without which we are incomplete. But Hazo's category of human love as the desire for complementarity is strained beyond its capacity in dealing with God's love. For it is important to recall that Kierkegaard emphasized God's unchangeableness in love. God is not altered by human response to love. God does not need to complete himself; God is complete. Although God seeks by love to cause us to love and become like God, this does not imply any deficiency in God.

It is in considering the incarnation that we reach a second under-

72

standing of God's love for us. God does not love us so much because we are similar to God, for we are not. Neither does God love us because we complement God, for we do not. But God's love creates the possibility of similarity, of becoming like God through the imitation of Christ. That love is not initiated by the perception of our likeness to God: it is sheer benevolence.

As the transforming power of God's love changes those who respond into a renewed likeness to God, the model by which we understand that love must also change. The benevolence which first sought to complete the incomplete in us now addresses itself benevolently to the new similarity. This is not to say that the Christian is similar to God in all respects, for obviously that is not the case. But as the Christian moves by imitating Christ to become more like God, the model for understanding God's love must expand to include similarity. God continues to complete us with the benevolence desire of complementarity, but also loves us for the ways in which we have become like God.

This does not imply, however, that God's love changes from the desire for complementarity to the desire of similarity. Rather as the person changes, our understanding of the love changes. We note here that we are employing categories for human love beyond the bounds for which they were developed.

Thus we can see how the love of God which seeks us out and makes us like God, despite its strong goal orientation, remains within the model of disinterested benevolence.

So far we have considered God's love under the category of tendency, mainly because Kierkegaard's account of divine love fits so well in these categories. But there are two reason for noting that divine cognition (Hazo's category of love as judgment) also has a part in divine love.

First, God's love must not be conceived separately from God's knowing, else we begin to think of God in ways that divide the divine nature. God does not think without loving or love without thinking, for God is love. While tendential and judgmental aspects of love can be separated on the human level because of the divided aspect of the human condition, our understanding of the divine nature dare not be formulated with such division. If cognitive categories of love are applicable to divine love, they must be in harmony with the tendential categories we have already reviewed.

Secondly, we are prompted to assume such cognitive categories, since divine love is the spring which supplies human love and, as we shall see below, Kierkegaard posits cognitive aspects of human love. Thus, from human cognitive love we look to its source in divine cognitive love, seeking the type of cognitive love which is in harmony with the tendential aspects we have already explored.

In Hazo, the judgment of love which elicits desire, and is thus necessarily joined with tendential love, is called "valuation."

73

When someone is so valued, he is seen as a person either from whom we want or for whom we seek something, as the means of getting what we want or as the recipient of what we want to give. This evaluative judgment of another gives rise to a desire in regard to him or causes a desire to be directed toward him. (48)

The source of the desire to benefit humanity in his love is the divine judgment of value. In contrast to the judgment of esteem, where love recognizes either some special or some intrinsic good in the beloved, benevolent valuation means simply that the beloved is valuable enough to the lover to want to give a good. Thus in God's love the benevolent judgment of worth in humanity issues in the benevolent desire to complete humanity's incompleteness and restore the divine likeness. Although Kierkegaard does not explore in detail God's love, the categories which we have just reviewed are not incompatible with his views. Since divine love is the source of human love, and since some human love includes cognitive aspects, the consideration of the cognitive aspect of God's love as valuation is a reasonable extension of Hazo's categories to Kierkegaard's view of divine love.

We now take up the question of human love toward God. We love God because God provides for a deficiency in us, restores the divine image in us, and this acquisitive desire in us continues, for we are always incomplete without God. But as we are re-created and made whole through grace and begin to imitate and grow toward a likeness of God, the question arises of the possibility of a love of similarity.

Would Kierkegaard agree that, as we grow in likeness to God, our love changes from the desire for complementarity to the desire of similarity? Would he accept the latter, even if the desire of similarity were acquisitive, i.e., the desire to benefit ourselves by relating to the other who is similar to us? We would guess not. Although the categories through which we have been exploring love would allow formally for such possibility, we suspect that Kierkegaard would see this as sheer presumption. Although formally it should be just as possible for us to love with desire for complementarity in those things wherein we have become like (as we have seen above in God's love for us), Kierkegaard's strong sense of the transcendance of God and our dependence upon God would emphasize the desire to be complemented far to the exclusion of the desire of similarity.

Kierkegaard commented in the Journals that the likeness to God into which we are transformed has its limitations:

The law of loving is quite simple and familiar; to love is to be transformed into likeness to the beloved.

Aber, aber,--this law holds only on the ascending and not on the descending scale. Example. If someone is superior in understanding and wisdom, the law for his love in relation to a person far inferior in understanding and wisdom is certainly not that he be transformed into likeness with the latter.* (49)

The asterisk leads to an entry in the margin:

Note: Of course it must be remembered that any conceivable superiority in the relation between man and man is still only a very imperfect analogy to the relation between being God and being human. (50)

We are therefore cautioned not to claim the latitude for our love to God that we see in God's love ot us. While God loves us with the desire to complete deficiencies in us with respect to that condition and with the love of similarity with respect to those conditions where we have become like God, our love to God does not go beyond the acquisitive desire to be fulfilled in God. Between human and divine love there remains an infinite qualitative difference.

We have seen in Kierkegaard's concept of Christian love the possibility of disinterested benevolence through divine aid. Having explored the judgemental aspects of divine benevolence, we now ask if judgment enters into Christian love for others, combining with the tendential aspects we have already reviewed.

In a brief section on Kierkegaard, Hazo holds up his distinction between love that has supernatural aid and love which does not. Kierkegaard states that admiration is a part of "earthly" love, i.e., love which does not accept the empowerment of Christ. (51) Christian love, however, is not based on admiration or any other preference; it is based on the commandment to love. Hazo identifies the cognitive aspect of Christian love with respect, the perception of the worth of another, not due to special qualities but due to his or her essential humanity. (52)

Whereas Hazo is definitely correct in denying that Christian love is based on admiration, the assertion that his category of respect is the appropriate one for Christian love lacks documentation. We recall that the categories of admiration and respect connote the cognitive aspects of a love which does not necessarily elict desire. Remembering that valuation can be combined with benevolence as the desire to benefit the one who is valued, it would seem that it also could be a part of Christian love. Kierkegaard has said, for example, that love for spouse and family does not cease in Christian love. Since these cases necessarily contain desire, we see that at least some Christian love should be categorized as valuation.

Furthermore, Kierkegaard points out that Christian love for all, including those who would not be loved by preference, is to desire for them a good:

But in love to hope all things signifies the lover's relationship to other men, that in relationship to them, hoping for them, he continually keeps possibility open with infinite partiality for his possibility of the good. Consequently he hopes in love that possibility is present at every moment, that the possibility of the good is present for the other person. . . . (53)

For Kierkegaard this hope or desire includes the possibility of blessedness, of becoming more like God, which is the highest good we can desire for ourselves or another.

Therefore, dissenting from Hazo at this point, we find that the desire laden category of valuation to be the most appropriate cognitive quality to combine with the benevolent desire of Christian love.

The Christian's love for others has been transformed so that cognitive and non-cognitive aspects are unified. A Christian can thus desire the good for another in an unselfish way. Loving in the imitation of God's love, the Christian values those whom God values, and this valuation is understood by the Christian in the commandment to love. Thus both the desire and the understanding of the Christian are combined in the enterprise of benevolence. Love continues to be a desire, i.e., an inclination to act coming from within the Christian, but that "within" has been transformed, unified. The Christian's desire is directed by the understanding that others are valuable, not because they are beautiful or lovable, but because they are valued by God. Hazo's category of "valuation," therefore, appropriately describes the Christian love of others.

We conclude this section by emphasizing again the connection between love for God and love for others.

For, Christianly understood, to love human beings is to love God and to love is to love human beings; what you do unto men you do unto God, and therefore what you do unto men God does unto you. (54)

And it is in the love which comes from God that the possibility of human benevolence lies.

NOTES
CHAPTER VI

(1) Louis Mackey, Kierkegaard: A Kind of Poet, p. 143.

(2) Søren Kierkegaard, The Point of View for My Work as an Author, p. 13.

(3) Louis Mackey, Kierkegaard: A Kind of Poet, pp. 226, 227.

(4) Søren Kierkegaard, The Point of View for My Work as an Author, p. 12.

(5) Søren Kierkegaard, Concluding Unscientific Postscript, p. 354.

(6) Ibid., p. 400.

(7) Ibid., p. 469.

(8) Ibid., p. 494.

(9) Ibid., p. 511.

(10) Ibid., p.545.

(11) Søren Kierkegaard, Philosophical Fragments, trans. with commentary by Howard Hong (Princeton, N.J.: Princeton University Press, 1971), p. 72.

(12) Søren Kierkegaard, Works of Love, p. 28.

(13) Ibid., p. 27.

(14) Søren Kierkegaard, Søren Kierkegaard's Journals and Papers Vol. 3, edited and translated by Howard and Edna Hong (Bloomington and London: Indiana University Press, 1975), p. 35.

(15) Ibid., p. 39.

(16) Ibid., p. 57.

(17) Ibid., p. 54.

(18) Ibid.

(19) Ibid., p. 38.

(20) Søren Kierkegaard, Philosophical Fragments, p. 30.

(21) Ibid., pp. 30, 31.

(22) Ibid., p. 39.

(23) Søren Kierkegaard, Christian Discourses and The Lilies of the Field and the Birds of the Air and Three Discourses at the Communion on Fridays, trans. with Introduction by Walter Lowrie (Princeton: Princeton University Press, 1971), p. 197.

(24) Søren Kierkegaard, Søren Kierkegaard's Journals and Papers Vol. 3, p. 33.

(25) Ibid., p. 58.

(26) Ibid., p. 57.

(27) Ibid., p. 49.

(28) Ibid., p. 53.

(29) Ibid., p. 47.

(30) Ibid., p. 48.

(31) Søren Kierkegaard, Works of Love, p. 33.

(32) Ibid., p. 40.

(33) Ibid., p. 47.

(34) Ibid., p. 65.

(35) Ibid., p. 67

(36) Ibid., p. 70

(37) Ibid., pp. 79, 80.

(38) Ibid., p. 133.

(39) Ibid., p. 158.

(40) Ibid., p. 255.

(41) Ibid., p. 261.

(42) Ibid., p. 262.

(43) Ibid., pp. 325, 326.

(44) Ibid., p. 267.

(45) Ibid., p. 269.

(46) Ibid., p. 274.

(47) Søren Kierkegaard, Edifying Discourses, trans. by David F. and Lillian Marvin Swenson, ed. by Paul Holmer (New York: Harper and Brothers Publishers, 1958), p. 59.

(48) Robert Hazo, The Idea of Love, p. 35.

(49) Søren Kierkegaard, Søren Kierkegaard's Journals and Papers Vol. 3, p. 56.

(50) Ibid., p. 58.

(51) Robert Hazo, The Idea of Love, p. 455.

(52) Ibid.

(53) Søren Kierkegaard, <u>Works of Love</u>, p. 237.

(54) <u>Ibid.</u>, pp. 351, 352.

Chapter VII
Aesthetic And Ethical Love
Religiously Considered

Aesthetic Love

Johannes de silentio observed in Fear and Trembling that outwardly it is difficult to distinguish the knight of faith from those on the aesthetic level. It is instructive in this regard to review the life of Kierkegaard, who considered himself as one on the religious level, but whose "public life" resembles part of the aesthetic works.

In 1837 Kierkegaard met Regina Olsen, when he was twenty-four and she was fourteen. Three years later, after an intense courtship, they were engaged. But immediately he decided that the engagement was a mistake. She seemed to him to be too spontaneous, innocent, and unreflective, in contrast to his persistent melancholy. He considered simply attempting to take her as a concubine, or marrying her without revealing to her the source of his disposition, but did neither. Instead he began to behave in an outrageous manner, so that Regina would believe him to be a deceiver and would be forced to break the engagement herself. Finally, in October of 1841, Kierkegaard himself broke the engagement.

Yet during a stay in Berlin, while writing Fear and Trembling and Repetition, the hope rekindled in Kierkegaard that, having renounced his life's love, it might be restored to him on a higher level. This was in line with the works in progress, where God rewarded the faithful Abraham and Job by returning to them what they had lost. The ending of Repetition, however, had to be changed to reflect the fact that the actual family of Job could not be restored, for Kierkegaard discovered that Regina had become engaged to her former admirer, Fritz Schlegel.

Thus we see many of the elements of Kierkegaard's personal love story in the previously reviewed cycle of seduction/broken engagement stories: a simple girl wooed by a complex and melancholy man with poetic tendencies, serious divergence between the two in religious sensibilities, the attempt to force responsibility for breaking the engagement on the girl, the question of how calculating reflection is like seduction.

As we consider aesthetic love from the vantage point of the religious level, therefore, we must not assume that distinctions will be outwardly apparent. Kierkegaard has emphasized that love on the religious level is hidden. It may therefore appear on occasions to be aesthetic love. Although Kierkegaard placed himself on the religious level, we see in his own love story an illustration of the difficulty of outwardly distinguishing between the religious and other levels. The real distinction is in the "inwardness" of the respective levels.

From the religious level, we can perceive the acquisitive nature of all aesthetic love. For example, not only is the love of Don Juan, Faust, and Johannes the Seducer acquisitive, but also the love of Donna Elvira, Margaret, and Cordelia. Although the aesthetic lover may be convinced that he or she loves with sacrificial concern for the beloved, from the religious level this can be seen as also self-oriented and acquisitive. As the aesthetic lover, I sacrifice for my beloved, and always with the hope that my beloved will respond in love to me.

It is this self-orientation of aesthetic and all other forms of preferential love which love on the religious level calls into question. Since God is love and the source of all love, the truest form of love is the love of neighbor which he commands. But this love does not have its roots in the agenda of the self. Rather, grounded in the sacrificial love of God, religious love is sacrificial love for neighbor, whether the neighbor be family, friend, stranger, or even enemy. The preferential nature of erotic aesthetic love does not have this range, for it is tied to the needs of the self.

From the vantage point of the religious level, this limited perspective of aesthetic love can be seen. Aesthetic love may see its unhappiness as accidental: one makes an unfortunate choice in love. The ethical level can see that the despair of aesthetic love is more than accidental, for in aesthetic love the possibility for happiness is always external, and is thus never secure. But only on the religious level is despair seen as sin, "the sickness unto death."

Sin is this: before God, or with the conception of God, to be in despair at not willing to be oneself, or in despair at willing to be oneself. Thus sin is potentiated weakness or potentiated defiance; sin is the potentiation of despair. The point upon which the emphasis rests is before God, or the fact that the conception of God is involved; . . . (1)

Anti-Climacus offers us an analysis of the despair which we have seen in aesthetic love. Recalling the correlation between despair and dread as aspects of the same phenomenon treated respectively under the category of will and consciousness, Anti-Climacus explores despair under the aspect of consciousness.

At the lowest level are those who are unconscious that they are in despair. This spiritlessness is seen in those figures of the immediate stages of the erotic: the melancholy page in Figaro, the bubbly love of Papageno in The Magic Flute, and finally in Don Juan. In the latter, love is characterized as woman-chasing desire, but with no reflection on the self as lover. All of the energy of love is poured into obtaining the favors of the desired one, with no recognition that he frantically seeks in the other the self he lacks.

The characters in The First Love also reflect this lack of consciousness of despair. Each has an agenda to pursue which has nothing to do with realizing full selfhood: securing a good marriage for a daughter, gaining financial support, obtaining a generous dowry, and maintaining nominal loyalty to "first love." Although they leave the stage with these goals attained, they are unknowingly in despair, for they do not know that they are selves who could despair.

The aesthetic level can only determine that love is happy or unhappy, and that there are varying degrees of self-consciousness. To see despair in terms of the will to be a self requires the perspective of another level:

No, it is not the aesthetic definition of spiritlessness which furnishes the scale for judging what is despair and what is not; the definition which must be used is the ethico-religious: either spirit/or the negative lack of spirit, spiritlessness. (2)

When the lover is conscious that he or she is in despair, the despairing love can take two forms. The first is to be in despair at not willing to be oneself, the "despair of weakness." This may be caused by something earthly, as in the case of an unhappy love affair, where blissful immediacy in love is broken by rejection and desertion. Such is the case of the women in "Shadowgraphs," whose immediacy is disturbed by faithless lovers. Lacking the strength to resolve their unhappiness by decision to move forward in life, they remain caught in the despair of weakness.

This is pure immediacy, or else an immediacy which contains a quantitative reflection.—Here there is no infinite consciousness of the self, of what despair is, or of the fact that the condition is one of despair; the despair is passive, succumbing to the pressure of the outward circumstance, it by no means comes from within the action. (3)

The despair of weakness may also be prompted by concern over the relationship of the self and the eternal. Here it is actually despair over one's weakness:

... he becomes now more clearly conscious of his despair, recognizing that he is in despair about the eternal, he despairs over himself that he could be weak enough to ascribe to the earthly such great importance, which now becomes his despairing expression for the fact that he has lost the eternal and himself. (4)

The despair of weakness concerning the self and the eternal, perhaps a less known kind, is to be seen in the figure of Faust described previously, as he throws himself into life:

In the latter case such a despairer will then plunge into life, perhaps into the distractions of great undertakings, the will become a restless spirit which leaves only too clear a trace of its actual presence, a restless spirit which wants to forget, and inasmuch as the noise within is so loud stronger means are needed. . . . Or he will seek forgetfulness in sensuality, perhaps in debauchery, in desperation he wants to return to immediacy, but constantly with consciousness of the self, which he does not want to have. (5)

In just such a sense Faust moved from his studies to Margaret to debauchery, despairingly in pursuit of the eternal which eluded him.

The despair at not willing to be oneself is contrasted by the despair of willing despairingly to be oneself. If the first were the despair of weakness, the second is the despair of defiance. Here there is a perception of the eternal in the self, the dawning of spirit. But the self does not respond to this perception by despairing of its own ability to gain the eternal, by losing itself in order to gain itself as a gift of the eternal. Rather the person wills to be a self in defiance of the need for the eternal, denying the Power which posits it.

In this form of despair there is now a mounting consciousness of the self, and hence greater consciousness of what despair is and of the fact that one's condition is that of despair. Here despair is conscious of itself as a deed, it does not come from without as a suffering under the pressure of circumstances, it comes directly from the self. And so after all defiance is a new qualification added to despair over one's weakness. (6)

This defiance may take an active form, acknowledging no power over it, as in the case of Johannes the Seducer, where calculating interaction with Cordelia shows that he is shut off from real love. He is conscious of himself but will not permit another to guide him into accepting the self he has been given. Rather in the isolation of his mind he constructs plans to alter another while he remains untouched. He will only be the self which he decides to be, but this is not a true self, since it does not relate to the Power which posits it.

The despair of willing to be oneself despairingly also takes a passive form, when one who suffers wills to remain in suffering.

But the more consciousness there is in such a sufferer who in despair is determined to be himself, all the more does despair too potentiate itself and become demoniac. The genesis of this is commonly as follows. A self which in despair is determined to be itself winces at one pain or another which simply cannot be taken away or separated from its concrete self. Precisely upon this torment the man directs his whole passion, which at last becomes a demoniac rage. Even if at this point God in heaven and all his angels were to offer to help him out of it--no, now he doesn't want it. . . . (7)

An example of this passivity in despair is to be seen in Quidam, who suffers because he is too melancholy to carry through on his engagement. He understands himself as religious, but does not seek God's help for a personal transformation which could allow love to grow. Rather he elects to remain in his suffering, renouncing his love in the name of a God whom he does not entreat. Thus his author, Frater Taciturnus, has described him as more demonic than religious.

From the vantage point of the religious level, all aesthetic love is in despair. Paradoxically, it is self-oriented, while at the same time lacking a true self. Indeed, aesthetic love attempts to gain a self without paying the price. It attempts to relate to another without relating to itself. It avoids the dialectic of self relating to its own self, denying that the self is a synthesis which must be willed. Images of "falling" in love, being "hopelessly" in love, are precisely indicative of the avoidance of the decision to constitute oneself as a self.

From the religious level this avoidance can be seen as sin, for aesthetic love does not submit itself to God for judgment and sustenance. When Christian love calls aesthetic love into question, therefore, it is not on the basis of the object of love. A young swain or maiden, a spouse, or a friend are as appropriate on the religious level as on the aesthetic. But Christian love submits the beloved to God, loves the beloved through God. Through God, Christian love loves all as neighbor--sweetheart, spouse, stranger, and enemy.

Aesthetic immediacy in love, therefore, is an avoidance of the mediation of God in love. It is the attempt to love independently from love's source and power. The lack of benevolence in aesthetic love is thus tied to its immediacy. As aesthetic love wills to remain in immediacy, it alienates itself from the source of benevolence, the love of God. And this precisely is the sin of aesthetic love.

Ethical Love

The ethical level also knows of despair and can perceive despair even more clearly than the aesthetic level. The ethicist perceives that in aesthetic love the condition for happiness is always outside oneself, thus sharing with the religious level a sensitivity to the despair over the earthly. The ethicist can even counsel the decision to despair, to choose oneself, to come to take an active responsibility in the relationship of the aspects which constitute the self.

But the ethical level does not relate despair to God, does not understand that despair is a religious category, that despair is sin. When a person understands that all of existence has reference to God, then despair is the unwillingness to find one's happiness in God, and this precisely is sin.

Although the ethical level knows of God and the ethicist feels comfortable that God provides the basis for the universal, the focus of the ethical level is the self. This is to be seen in Judge William's equation of choosing despair and choosing self, which means choosing to be a self. It is also to be seen in the definition of Socrates, the great prototype of the ethical. For Socrates, sin is ignorance. His ethic proceeds from the confidence that one who knows the good will do the good. The self is thus able in an unproblematic way to assimilate the necessary knowledge and respond appropriately.

But Christianity understands that sin is not in the intellect but in the will.

Socrates explains that he who does not do the right thing has not understood it; but Christianity goes a little further back and says, it is because he will not understand it, and this in turn is because he does not will the right. And in the next place, describing what properly is defiance, it teaches that a man does wrong although he understands what is right, or forbears to do right although he understands what is right; in short, the Christian doctrine of sin is pure impertinence against man, accusation upon accusation; it is the charge which the Deity as prosecutor takes the liberty of lodging against man. (8)

From the perspective of the religious level, it is the reference of all existence to God which distinguishes it from the ethical. The ethical in its heightened self-consciousness may choose the self in relation to the Universal, but it does not see that God is above the ethical, that God is sovereign over the ethical.

Happiness by earthly standards, or even correctness by ethical standards, is not the goal on the religious level, for God is above all. This realization intrudes upon the ethical level in Either/Or II with the "Ultimatum: The Edification Implied in the Thought that as against God We are always in the Wrong."

Not surprisingly, the point of the "Ultimatum" is made by reference to love:

Your life brings you into manifold relationships with other people, to some of whom you are drawn by a more heartfelt love than you feel for others. Now if such a man who was the object of your love were to do you a wrong, it would pain you deeply, would it not? You would carefully rehearse everything that had occurred--but then would you say, I know of myself that I am in the right, this thought shall tranquilize me? (9)

No, the exercise continues, it is better to consider oneself in the wrong. It is less painful to believe that you have erred than to believe that your beloved friend is in the wrong. So one is strengthened by the approach that, in conflict with the beloved, one is always in the wrong.

How much more so is this the case when the beloved is God!

So it is an edifying thought that against God we are always in the wrong. If this were not the case, if this conviction did not have its source in your whole being, that is, did not spring from the love within you, then your reflection also would have taken a different turn; . . . (10)

On the ethical level it would be possible to deliberate under the categories of right and wrong, to determine whether the lover or the beloved were right, but on the religious level ultimate reference is not made to right. It is made to God. Such was the case with Abraham, who bypassed the ethical in response to the divine command. Although on the ethical level he was condemned for the willingness to sacrifice his beloved son, his action reflected the maxim that "against God we are always in the wrong."

On the religious level all is related to God. The benevolence with which we are called to love is God's gift, and therefore all our love is mediated by God. Yet, could not the ethicist say the same? Indeed, did not Judge William emphasize that love was a divine gift, that married people should consider their spouses as given to them by God?

The distinction, then, between love on the ethical and religious levels is not that love is given and mediated by God, for Judge William's position evolved to emphasize divine mediation also. Rather the distinction lies in that, on the religious level, all of life is referred at every moment to God. The ethical is too at home in the world to consider that the ethic which evolved out of thoughtful consideration of the universal might still be in conflict with divine will. Thus the necessity of the intrusion of the "Ultimatum." For Judge William cannot see how the ethical can be against God.

The first movement beyond the ethical understanding of love is seen in religiousness A. Since love on the ethical is seen as a harmonious continuity, resignation of earthly love in favor of the love for God is unthinkable. Likewise, the possibility that loving God could make one unhappy and that suffering could be an essential characteristic of the Christian faith does not occur to ethical love. Finally, although Judge William has been exposed to the possibility of guilt before God in the "Ultimatum," it has not significantly changed his outlook. Thus the three characteristics of religiousness A are alien to an ethical perspective on love. The passionate intensity and problematic nature of existence on this level would probably appear to Judge William as the arrested development of aesthetic love.

To be in love for half a year and stand ready to risk everything--that we can readily understand. But then at last, one must surely be permitted to wed the damsel, and stretch one's weary limbs in the privileged marriage-bed. . . But the absolute _telos_ exists for the individual only when he yields it an absolute devotion. And since an eternal happiness is a _telos_ for existing individuals, these two (the absolute end and the existing individual) cannot be conceived as realizing a union in existence in terms of rest. This means that an eternal happiness cannot be possessed in time, as the youth and the maiden may possess one another, both being existing individuals. But what this means, namely, that they cannot be united in time, every lover readily understands. It means that the whole of time is here the period of courtship. (11)

In comparison to the absolute relation to the absolute, marriage, the model of ethical love, is a "jest." (12) For the husband and wife are not related absolutely to one another on the level of religiousness A. They are related relatively to each other and each absolutely to God.

In contrast to the lengthy descriptions of married love offered by Judge William religiousness A knows that absolute passion is inexpressible:

Absolute passion cannot be understood by a third party, and this holds both for his relationship to others and for their relationship to him. In absolute passion the individual is in the very extremity of his subjectivity, as a consequence of his having reflected himself out of every external relativity; but a third party is precisely such a relativity. (13)

The level of religiousness B is also contrasted to the ethical in regard to love. We recall that here that temporal existence is paradoxically affirmed as the setting where the conditions for eternal happiness are given. But because of the objective uncertainty of any historical event, faith demands that the condition of eternal happiness (that God was in the lowly Jesus suffering and dying for us) be appropriated subjectively with passionate intensity. Thus faith is like a woman who hears that she has been loved:

If a woman who is in love were to receive at second hand the assurance that the man she loved (who was dead and from whose mouth she had never heard the assurance) had affirmed that he loved her--let the witness or witnesses be the most reliable of men, let the case be so plain that a captious and incredulous lawyer would say it is certain--the lover will at once detect the precariousness of this report; it is hardly a compliment to the woman to suppose that she would not, for objectivity is no crown of honor for a lover. (14)

The reference to the lawyer in the above section and to the court system in a subsequent example carry an implied message for the ethical Judge William. The methodical rationality of the ethical does not apply on the level of paradoxical religiousness.

In religiousness B the temporal sphere of existence takes on a new importance. Religiousness A knows how to resign the temporal and relative in favor of the absolute relation to the divine, but this highest level knows how it is possible to love the earthly beloved through one's love for God. On the paradoxical level one gives up the beloved, but through faith may yet receive the beloved back again. The ethical level would tend to deny the necessity of this whole dialectic.

(1) Søren Kierkegaard, <u>Fear</u> <u>and</u> <u>Trembling</u>/<u>Sickness</u> <u>Unto</u> <u>Death</u>, p. 208.

(2) <u>Ibid</u>., p. 179.

(3) <u>Ibid</u>., p. 184.

(4) <u>Ibid</u>., p. 195.

(5) <u>Ibid</u>., p. 199.

(6) <u>Ibid</u>., p. 201.

(7) <u>Ibid</u>., p. 205.

(8) <u>Ibid</u>., p. 226.

(9) Søren Kierkegaard, <u>Either</u>/<u>Or</u> <u>II</u>, p. 349.

(10) <u>Ibid</u>., p. 353.

(11) Søren Kierkegaard, <u>Concluding</u> <u>Unscientific</u> <u>Postscript</u>, p. 355.

(12) <u>Ibid</u>., p. 408.

(13) <u>Ibid</u>., p.454.

(14) <u>Ibid</u>., p. 511.

Chapter VIII
Issues In Kierkegaard's
Concept Of Love

Thus far we have looked at love within the Kierkegaardian framework of the three levels of existence. We have used Hazo's description of the categories of love as a springboard to analysis. It is now time to take an overview of Kierkegaard's presentation of love on the three levels, noting the relationship of love on the various levels, the scope of tendencies and judgments which fall under the notion of love, and the areas of love which Kierkegaard did not explore. For the purpose of this evaluation, we begin with three approaches to the relationship between eros and agape.

Three Views of Eros and Agape

From the Pauline use of agape Anders Nygren draws a set of characteristics of the term. First: Agape is spontaneous and "unmotivated" by the value of its object. Second: It is "indifferent to value" in the object of love. Third: It is creative of value in the object of love. Fourth: It initiates fellowship with God. (1) Agape is primarily God's love for humanity and secondarily the Christian's love for others. Since the human response to divine love is motivated and reflective of the supreme value of God, Paul has rightly, according to Nygren, reserved the term "faith" for this response, thus preserving the above characteristics for agape.

Nygren laments, however, that other New Testament writers, even the writer of the sublime Johannine material on love, were not so careful with the term. Here he sees the entrance of another motif into the Christian tradition, the love known as eros.

Eros, the love of the beautiful and good, has three primary characteristics: First: It is acquisitive. Second: It is the human path to the divine, operating in the sharp dualism between the heavenly and the earthly. Third: It is egocentric, seeking the happiness of the self. (2) Given its classic form by Plato, eros is to be seen entering the Christian tradition, according to Nygren, when the strict Pauline definition of agape is qualified in any way. He sees an example of this in the discussion of the appropriateness of various objects for Christian love, for Pauline agape is not characterized by its object. This "fall" of Christianity into the sway of eros is seen to culminate in Augustine's caritas, where Christian love is identified as the acquisitive desire for the eternal happiness of the soul.

When eros and agape are defined in these ways, they could hardly be more sharply opposed. Indeed, from Nygren's perspective, we see two absolutely opposite inclinations called by the same English word--"love."

Denis de Rougemont in Love in the Western World has advanced a far reaching theory concerning romantic love which makes an interesting correlation with our exploration of love in the work of Kierkegaard. In tracing the characteristics of romantic (non-married) love through the story of Tristan and Iseult, he notes that romance thrives on impediments, and is intensified by that which bars sexual union and the normalization of the relationship in marriage. When romantic lovers lack an external impediment (distance, legal barriers, familial opposition, etc.), an impediment is provided nevertheless (spells, sense of obligation to another, etc.). The real goal of romance, de Rougemont concludes, is not to possess the beloved, not even to benefit the beloved. It is to inflame the lover.

> Passion means suffering, something undergone, the mastery of fate over a free and responsible person. To love love more than the object of love, to love passion for its own sake, has been to love to suffer and to court suffering all the way from Augustine's amabam amare down to modern romanticism. (3)

The goal of passion, he continues, is the self-awareness which comes about by suffering and the risk of death. Since happiness is not the goal, it should not surprise us that most of the archetypal romances are unhappy; the impediment remains. If romance resolves itself into consummation, the loss of impediment would lessen the intensity of the passion which romance seeks. The opportunity for self-understanding through passionate suffering would be denied.

The orientation, therefore, of passionate romance is not the beloved but the self:

> But unhappiness comes in, because the love which 'dominates' them is not a love of each for the other as that other really is. They love one another, but each loves the other from the standpoint of self and not from the other's standpoint. (4)

This self-orientation is to be seen in the description of romantic love itself, for what is described is not so much the virtue and beauty of the beloved as the intensity of passion in the lover.

De Rougemont goes on to correlate the passion of romance with the passion of mysticism, and the self-salvation doctrine of philosophical eros:

> We must ask ourselves if to understand through suffering is not the capital feature as well as the daring element in our most self-conscious mysticism. The two passions--the erotic (in a higher sense) and the mystical--speak one same language, whether because either is cause or effect of the other or because they have a common origin. . . . (5)

Without judging the merits of de Rougemont's historical analysis, his literary survey is instructive, resembling the reservations of Judge William concerning mysticism.

The erotic dualism of romance and mysticism is contrasted with Christian love. Instead of seeking to deny and finally flee the body in death, Christian love is a new beginning in physical and temporal life.

> But in Christianity, thanks to its dogma of the incarnation of the Christ in Jesus, this process is completely inverted. Death, from being the last term, is become the first condition. What the Gospel calls dying to self is the beginning of a new life already here below . . . . (6)

Thus the symbol of Christian love is not the infinite passion of the individual self seeking understanding through suffering. Rather it is the act of marriage, symbolized by the marriage of Christ to the Church, the finding of self in the context of fulfillment in earthly life. In so arguing, de Rougemont closely aligns himself with Judge William. We shall see later how he reckons with Kierkegaard's account of passion on the religious level.

M.C. D'Arcy evolves a third position on the relationship of eros and agape by way of formulating a critique of the two previous ones. Against Nygren he argues that it is impossible to remove all traces of self-concern from love. Nor is Nygren's distinction between nature and grace adequate:

> The point made here is that grace does not destroy all that is human; it perfects it and elevates it to a new dynamic, and the real problem is to work out how both nature and the supernatural life survive in their integrity in the Christian order. Nygren cuts the knot and sunders self-love and grace, nature and the supernatural completely. (7)

That both eros and agape are called by the name of "love" indicates that at least some common elements are perceived. Nygren's typology cannot account for this.

D'Arcy criticizes de Rougemont in much the same way. De Rougemont does not offer a model for the transformation of eros into agape, thus failing to show how the "passionate" language of mysticism is connected with Christianity.

> But a much more important difficulty is this, that de Rougemont allows for no kind of love in between the pagan passion of Eros and the Christian and supernatural love of charity. It would seem as if the world outside Christian love had to live by one desire alone, the desire to be free from this clogging world, to deny it and by death pass into fusion with the All. . . . There must in fact have been a quiet ordered love in all civilizations; one which lacked the specific and supernatural character of Christian Agape and yet preserved a balance and discipline. No civilization could live on the wild frenzy

which alone is mentioned and contrasted with the Christian ideal by de Rougemont. (8)

D'Arcy is not totally fair to de Rougemont at this point, for the latter has acknowledged the marriages of convenience and necessity which were characterized by neither eros nor agape. He simply denied the presence of love in these situations. But D'Arcy's point still has merit. Why should relationships which mingle passion with commitment outside the Christian context be denied the name of love? De Rougemont's typology cannot acocunt for this.

D'Arcy furthermore points out areas of disagreement between Nygren and de Rougemont on the meaning of eros:

> Whereas, then, de Rougemont considers Eros to be unrestrained and passionate, and, apparently, more inclined to self-effacement than to self-regard, Nygren defines it as an Hellenic ideal, as intellectual, self-complacement and possessive, as, in short, irretrievably ego-centric. (9)

(We noted when analyzing Kierkegaard's account of aesthetic love a surprising absence of eros as defined by de Rougemont according to the above description.)

In D'Arcy's view, human love necessarily has elements of egocentric concern, but also inevitably yearns for its completion through divine grace.

> By nature we are bound to consult the wellbeing of ourselves first, and we are inclined to give the regency to the intellect and to subject all other powers of the soul under it. But, as we know now, anima is always restless when under too severe duress of the intellect, for it has another love. This other love is the love which a human person as a person has for God, from whom he has his existence, and for others as persons. It is not egocentric because a person always spells a relation, and in that personal relation the centrifugal love finds vent. (10)

The dichotomy of eros and agape argued by Nygren and de Rougemont misses the point, then, that these loves are synthesized in human existence. Divine grace, working in the context of human eros, extends, exalts and perfects human love.

Each of the above views on the relationship between eros and agape is helpful in its own way, but finally inadequate to explain the complexity of that relationship. Nygren correctly identifies the ego-centric nature of eros and its contrast to the self-giving activity of agape. Because of the clear and explicit nature of this contrast, agape furnishes a basis for the Christian faith to call ego-centric eros into question. But in focusing only on the Pauline use of agape as normative for the meaning and content of agape, Nygren is vulnerable to the charge of being arbitrary. He does not and cannot defend why the Pauline use of agape is normative, while all other

New Testament uses are not.

De Rougemont is most helpful in two ways. First, he introduces another dimension of eros into the picture; the desire for the loss of self through passion and suffering. Nygren's account of the acquisitive nature of eros did not touch on this. De Rougemont injects into our inquiry the intense desire of the lover so to possess the beloved that he or she loses self in love. By showing the relationship between this passion and the impulse to save oneself by mystical assent, he reveals the ego-centric agenda behind the desire to lose self and thus provides a contrast with theocentric agape. He also is able to distinguish a kind of passion which is acceptable in the Christian context.

Secondly, de Rougemont includes in his consideration the implications of eros and agape for the love between men and women, and raises the Christian meaning of marriage. He shows how love which is based upon the concern for self is inadequate as a Christian expression and how agape is a fundamentally different kind of love. For agape, as a gift of God, is genuine concern for the beloved.

But this account of eros does not explain the reason some eros claims the object of desire, while other eros practices self-salvation by the denial of the object of desire. Why is some eros simply acquisitive while other eros desires (yet does not consummate) union? In de Rougemont eros becomes so identified with the latter that the simple reaching out and claiming the beloved hardly qualifies as eros at all. If the entry of religious dualism into Western consciousness is the key to understanding eros, as de Rougemont argues, what of the love which simply desires and claims its beloved?

D'Arcy rightly points out another deficiency. Typologies of love such as those of Nygren and de Rougemont fail to account for any middle ground, any mixture of eros and agape, any love which combines primacy of the self and primacy of the other. If eros and agape are so opposite, how can we account for the fact that they are both seen as love?

D'Arcy, then, counters with a model of love wherein the deficiency of eros as a kind of love is met with the fullness of grace-filled agape. Agape complements, completes, and transforms the ego-centric tendencies or eros. Human love becomes a synthesis of eros and agape.

The value of D'Arcy is that he explores the middle ground which is the common experience of human existence. Rather than resolving an example of love into one or the other side of the typology, as would Nygren or de Rougemont, he shows how eros and agape combine in existence as we experience it. But in so doing, D'Arcy gives up the sharp contrast between eros and agape which the former two authors had established. How can agape so readily combine with eros and still call it into question?

The initial promise and final inadequacy of these positions calls us to set forth criteria to evaluate the notion of love, which can then be used to evaluate Kierkegaard's writings. A valid Christian statement on love must at least contain the following strengths: (1) With Nygren and de Rougemont, it must sharply distinguish between ego-centric eros and self-giving agape. (2) With de Rougemont, it must explore the implications of eros and agape for male-female relationships, specifically in the matters of courtship, sexuality, celibacy, and marriage. (3) It must distinguish between the simple acquisitive eros described by Nygren and the self-losing eros described by de Rougemont, and yet show how both are properly called eros. (4) It must take account of the mixture of ego-centered love and self-giving love, which is the common experience of human existence. We shall now see how Kierkegaard's account of love on the three levels meets these criteria.

An Evaluation of Kierkegaard's Account of Love

Kierkegaard has sharply distinguished love based on the divine commandment to love and all forms of "preferential" love. Christian love is not based on human preference or the desirability of the beloved, but simply and fully on the love which God gives and empowers in each person. The impetus for Christian love, then, comes not from the human lover who finds himself or herself inclined to reach out to the beloved. The mysterious and unruly tendencies which characterize eros are surpassed. Agape is commanded by God and thus the impetus is from him. Christians love others, not because they are beautiful or lovable, but because they are first loved by God and then commanded to love others.

It is irrelevant, therefore, whether the other who is to be loved fits any agenda for the self. The beloved may be beautiful or ugly, admirable or despicable, friend or enemy. For Christian love is not characterized by the desires and inclinations which flow from the self. Christian love is characterized by its works, which are capable of being commanded in a way that desires are not.

For Kierkegaard God's love is sheer benevolence. It is a spontaneous act of God, flowing not because of the value of the beloved or of any gain to be derived by God. It cannot be explained by the beauty or worth of the object of love. Its motivation is a part of the mystery: God is love.

Thus Kierkegaard has articulated a view of God's love and the Christian's love of others which is close to that of Nygren and de Rougemont. Here love is not defined by the value of the beloved. It is motivated by the grace of divine love. The motivation of divine love cannot be attributed to the value of the object of love, for God's love creates value.

Kierkegaard has also noted that it is not possible to love God for his own sake. Our love of God is motivated; God has intrinsic value for us. We love him because he first loved us. Nygren made the same point by denying that it is possible to agape God, since he had defined agape as unmotivated love. But Kierkegaard finds himself in a better position than Nygren, for he has made the point without recourse to an arbitrary and restrictive definition, thus avoiding Nygren's favoring of the Pauline letters over the Gospels.

With Nygren and de Rougemont, Kierkegaard also holds that the benevolence of the Christian's love for others is possible only with divine aid. Even the examples of natural benevolence in a mother's love, which were provided by Judge William are open to question, for they are preferential love, and preferential love is ego-centric.

Kierkegaard's notion of the level and their relationships is helpful in distinguishing agape and eros, for he noted on several occasions that the goals and concerns of one level may be carried on to another, although qualitatively changed. This is another way of saying that persons loved in eros on one level could be loved in agape on the religious level. The beloved remains but love changes. This point is the sharpest possible way to the Kierkegaardian distinction between Christian and non-Christian love, elsewhere typed as agape and eros. Kierkegaard thus satisfies our first criterion: that agape and eros be sharply distinguished.

Concerning our second criterion for evaluating Kierkegaard on love, he has given us, perhaps even more than de Rougemont, an exploration of eros and agape in the relationship between men and women. Kierkegaard and de Rougemont would agree that a key issue in eros is that of self-consciousness. But de Rougemont does not offer a coherent model at this point. He rightly points out that eros needs an impediment and that that impediment is a catalyst in emerging self-consciousness for the lover. But he also maintains that the goal of eros is death, the loss of self-consciousness, without providing a model for how these two opposite tendencies are united in eros.

D'Arcy points out along this line that de Rougemont deals with one aspect of eros while Nygren deals with another:

Nygren, then, presents us with self love and its most powerful instrument, the human reason; de Rougemont presents us with a romantic and ecstatic love, which is either irrational or ill at ease at the superior claims upon it of reason. One love takes and posesses; the other love likes to be beside itself and give. One is masculine, the other is feminine. (11)

D'Arcy suggests that these two aspects of eros are a natural balance of human existence, with one or the other alternately coming to the fore in a cyclical fashion. Kierkegaard, on the other hand, would suggest that these aspects are sequential, and that they reflect different levels of self-consciousness which are not necessarily cyclical. He shows how eros draws lovers together, how on the lowest levels of immediacy they seek in the beloved the completion of the self which they have not fully attained. They are awakened to their incompleteness by the problem of a faithless lover. Here the unhappy lover may seek by eros to return to the lower levels of immediacy, paralleling de Rougemont's description of the quest for the loss of consciousness in death. Or the unhappy lover may move to a higher level of existence in the quest of greater self-consciousness. Or, finally, the unhappy lover may be frozen at the boundary between the aesthetic and the ethical. In its passive form, this involves the continued suffering from betrayal; in its active form the seduction of others. Thus the Kierkegardian construct of levels of existence provides what de Rougemont did not: a model to explain how eros could move either toward greater self-conscious modes or toward the loss of self-consciousness. Further, Kierkegaard seeks to invite a person in this situation into a posture of self-conscious reflection and choice, rather than offer with D'Arcy the consolation that these modes of love alternate and thus may be adopted at any time in the future.

Kierkegaard also explores the married relationship and the courtship leading to it. Judge William's project is to justify married love to those moved by eros on the aesthetic level, by showing how married love is more realistic and complete than aesthetic love. But in so doing, he meets eros on its own ground. Although he points to examples of benevolence in a mother's love and credits God with making love a gift, he does not distance marriage from the ego-centric agenda of eros. He simply shows how the agenda is completed more fully in marriage.

This in in contrast to de Rougemont, who grounds the faithfullness of marriage in agape. He argues that faithfullness in marriage needs no justification.

Forgoing any rationalist or hedonist form of apology I propose to speak only of a troth that is observed by virtue of the absurd--that is to say, simply because it has been pledged--and by virtue of being an absolute which will uphold husband and wife as persons. (12)

The love which characterizes Christian marriage, as de Rougemont sees it, is not evoked by the beauty or value of the beloved; it is grace-filled agape. That de Rougemont would forgo and Judge William would not forgo an apology to the aesthetic is the clue to their difference. Judge William's married love is a higher and more benevolent form of eros; de Rougemont married love is based on agape.

In his account of eros, de Rougemont finally has recourse to Kierkegaard himself.

And Kierkegaard is right over them all, because, first, he extolled passion as being the highest value in the 'aesthetic stage' of life; then rose above passion by extolling marriage as being the highest value in the 'ethical stage' (the 'fullness of time'); and finally condemned marriage as the highest obstruction in the 'religious state,' since marriage fetters us to time where faith requires eternity. (13)

He goes on to show how, with Kierkegaard, it is possible "by virtue of the absurd" to claim in agape the beloved who was removed in eros. Thus the Christian may marry as part of the commandment to love and may remain in marriage, not through preferential eros, but through grace-filled agape.

Kierkegaard, then, does indeed give a full account of eros and agape to the various relations between men and women as lovers. Furthermore, he is able to offer a model for distinguishing the different phenomena called by the name of eros.

Finally we must also evaluate Kierkegaard on how he explored those experiences of love which are not meaningfully resolved into opposing types of love. Included here are stable and loving marriages outside the Christian tradition. Also are experiences in which real disinterested benevolence is so intertwined with the rewards of the relationship that it would be impossible to distinguish between the ego-centric agenda of eros and the benevolent concern of agape. How can we account for the fact that both eros and agape are called "love" and that self-interest and benevolence can combine in such complex ways that precise differentiation is impossible?

Kierkegaard's discussion of these matters is not extensive. On the aesthetic level the description only involves ego-centric acquisitive love. On the religious level love is pure benevolence. Judge William's account of marriage claims the possibility of disinterested benevolence, but his description is not extensive. His examples, furthermore, could just as easily be considered self-interested benevolence, illustrating the point that some love is not amenable to typologies.

Our contention is simply that Kierkegaard's presentation of love has room to take account of this area because it is descriptive rather than analytical. His interest is not to resolve an example of love into a type or a polarity, but to allow the reader to find himself or herself in the experience he is describing. Here again the construct of three levels offers a welcome latitude which typologists such as Nygren and de Rougemont do not have.

Finally, in evaluating the capacity of Kierkegaard's work to account for love that cannot be resolved into eros or agape, it is important to remember that Kierkegaard saw God's love as the source of all human love. Not only the open-handed and clearly benevolent love in response to divine commandment, but also the self-interested benevolence of love for family, and even the immediacy of desire in reaching out for another, all are for Kierkegaard examples from which he does not withhold the designation of "love." Even as he calls preferential love into question on behalf of the commandment to love, the middle ground of love is present.

Points of Emphasis and Areas of Silence

As we have analyzed Kierkegaard's account of love on the various levels, we have noted, despite a wide range of description, certain areas of silence. It is now time to take an overview of the things Kierkegaard emphasized and those he did not.

On the aesthetic level, we observed two aspects of acquisitive love which were not explored. First, Kierkegaard seemed not to notice that romantic love often is articulated as the desire for the union of complementarity. We have noted that this desire may be acquisitive or benevolent, and thus could be in keeping with the acquisitive characterization of love on the aesthetic level.

The notion of romantic love as the desire to complete oneself in another would have fit nicely with Anti-Climacus' observations on the incompleteness of the self on the aesthetic level. Anti-Climacus had analyzed the deficiency of a self which does not recognize its synthetic nature and does not relate itself to itself. He has shown how the despair of those who avoid coming to recognition and acceptance of their full selfhood seek to distract themselves in love. It would have been a simple step to survey the desire for the union of complementarity and show how this meshed. Thus the often expressed romantic sentiment that the lover feels incomplete without the beloved could be seen as the avoidance of selfhood by relating in the beloved to another self. In this way a major theme in romantic love would have been explained by an important concept in the Kierkegaardian corpus.

This was not explicitly done in any breadth by Kierkegaard or his pseudonyms. Yet a related concept, that of immediacy in romantic love, was explored at length, and for this we will have to settle. On the aesthetic level immediacy is the spontaneous and unself-consciousness state of those who do not see themselves as a syntheses, do not relate self to self. The self as subject does not see the self as object.

Kierkegaard's dependable foil, Hegel, had seen in the history of humanity a movement from immediacy to self-consciousness, the state which was to be exemplified by his philosophy. Kierkegaard took over this concept of movement from immediacy to self-consciousness, but with several major changes. (1) It was seen as a phenomenon of the individual, not the masses. (2) It was made a matter of decision and will, not an inevitable movement. (3) Christianity was moved from a level of immediacy to the highest level of self-consciousness. Yet Kierkegaard kept the valuing of self-consciousness over immediacy, and built this into his structure of levels of existence.

Kierkegaard has described in detail the tendency to retreat from self-consciousness which characterizes the person in immediacy, and the way eros serves in this process by distracting the self from its lack of relation to itself. Thus the beloved of immediate erotic love provides a sense of completeness of self which is actually incomplete, and avoids the anxiety of incompleteness which could lead to self-consciousness, decision, and the relation of full selfhood. Thus immediate eros and the desire for the union of complementarity are the same love. Kierkegaard has given an account of love which would have been further enriched if he had made this implicit connection explicit.

A second aspect of romantic love which Kierkegaard did not explore is its often-stated claim of benevolence. The romantic lover proclaims willingness to sacrifice anything for the benefit of the beloved. At times this claim is the intentional deceit of a seducer, but it also may be the actual belief of the romantic lover. What is to be made of this claim?

As we have seen, Kierkegaard and his pseydonyms are aware of the ego-centric and acquisitive nature of romantic love. Especially from the religious level, the romantic choice of the beloved is seen to be a preference of the self. But even the pseudonym on the aesthetic account is on the acquisitive desire to possess the beloved. Only occasionally does love as the desire to benefit the beloved appear at all, and when it does, the primary aim is still the benefit of the lover. "A" specifically assigns benevolence to the ethical level, but seems to know nothing of the aesthetic claim for benevolence.

Let us admit that this is a gap in the Kierkegaardian corpus. The account would have been improved if the benevolent claim of romantic love had been analyzed in detail and refuted. But, as noted earlier, benevolent romantic love was so far from Kierkegaard's view that perhaps he could not explore but could only dismiss it.

On the ethical level we noted the continuity of love characterized as decision. Thus Judge William made marriage the model for love on the ethical level, stressing the continuity of ethical love and the joy which commitment brings.

We raised the question, when reviewing the judge's account of ethical love, of the place of God in his views. When he argued for a "second immediacy" in love following upon reflection and decision, he based this possibility as a gift of God, a miracle, for the entrance to the ethical is by the choice of self which banishes immediacy.

Although Kierkegaard seemed to be kindly disposed to his representative of the ethical love, he could not have agreed with his articulation of his faith. The doctrines of Trinity, Incarnation, Justification by faith, and the Resurrection are not discussed by the judge. Yet the concept of "second immediacy" shows that these transformational concepts are implicit in his thought.

In order to see how this is the case, let us shift the framework of the discussion from the judge's attempt to justify marriage to the aesthetic consciousness. Instead of the question being "How can there be immediacy in marriage?" let the question be posed: "How can we be so continually and closely involved with a marriage partner that reflection is not a threat to the intensity of love?". We must admit with the judge the necessity of the grace of God at this point. Without a transformation of consciousness, the conflict of immediacy versus reflection could not be resolved. It is only the self which relates to self by dying to self and being raised in Christ which resolves this contradiction.

On the aesthetic level, the ethical level, and even that of religiousness A, Judge William's second immediacy does not succeed in breaking free from the dilemma as he has set it up. The place where "second immediacy" makes sense is religiousness B, where the transforming resources of the Christian faith come into view. For those who died to self and live in Christ reflection is not the enemy of the passion of faith but the vehicle of that passion. Love becomes, not the quest for the perfect aesthetic experience, but the transformation through suffering into the likeness of the Christ who

101

loved all. In this context reflection on the relationship between oneself and the beloved is not the end of intensity of love. It is its true beginning.

We may take it as a mark of Kierkegaard's kindly disposition toward the judge that he allows him implicitly to be graced by the transforming power of specifically Christian love. But what of others living on the ethical level? What, for example, of non-Christians? Despite the sharp contrast which Kierkegaard was wont to draw between Christianity and all levels below it, would he agree that others on the ethical level could experience the continually renewed intensity of love which the judge called "second immediacy"?

Without attempting a definitive answer here, we would guess that Kierkegaard might hold out the possibility of immediacy, but in a limited sense. When the judge recognizes that "second immediacy" is really mediation by God, he is approaching Kierkegaard's own statement that Christians move to love out of God's commandment to love rather than personal reference. Christians love the neighbor--the one who is given to them to love, in a similar sense to the way a married person loves the spouse who is God's gift. Thus the loss of concern for self in the passion of Christian love has a formal similarity to the passion of immediacy as Judge William describes it. From these considerations we would guess that Kierkegaard would agree that God grants even to non-Christians the gift of intensity in married love.

Judge William's picture of benevolence on the ethical level must also be reviewed. We have already seen that the judge would not have made the sharp distinction between mixed acquisitive desire and self-interested benevolence, for he saw a continuity of love on the ethical level. But he did see possibility of disinterested benevolence within a general pattern of self-interested benevolence. In a sense this benevolence is supernaturally aided, because of the continuum which moves from self-interest to disinterest and which is made possible by God. Yet we miss any account of the way divine love specifically transforms and empowers human love to move into true benevolence.

Using the language of Anti-Climacus, the married lover has chosen himself or herself by relating self to self, and by this act bringing about the synthesis which selfhood demands. But we do not see in any detail an understanding that the self must also relate to the power of God which finally is the constitutive factor of the self. Of course it could be argued as in the previous case that Kierkegaard has allowed a specifically Christian characteristic to find its way into the ethical level. But Kierkegaard himself calls Judge William's highest example of benevolence into question: ". . . maternal love as such is simply self-love raised to a higher power, . . . (14) The ethical level lacks the category of growth in grace which has been the experience of Christianity down through the centuries. We are not surprised that the judge's examples of disinterested benevolence are open to question. The dynamics of supernatural aid and human intent are too vague on the ethical level to explain how self is truly transcended in love. Yet we do note a movement from the aesthetic to the ethical level. Ethical love is able at least to be concerned primarily with the good of the beloved and only the good of the self as a secondary goal, a capacity we did not find on the aesthetic level.

It is finally love on the religious level which offers the basis for clarity concerning love on the preceeding levels. Here the identification of love with immediacy on the aesthetic level and the uncritical assumption of benevolence on the ethical level come up against the more profound immediacy of love for God and the true benevolence which springs from that immediacy.

Of central interest to us on the religious level is the concept that love to God implies the attempt to become like him through the imitation of Christ. As a unifying theme, the imitation of Christ involves suffering and a weaning away from the values of the world. It means loving others in the manner that God loves, not for beauty or value to self, but because that love is commanded by the God who is beloved.

Although the ethical level could place God in a mediating role in love, particularly married love, the religious level goes a step further. That God is the "middle term" in love on the religious level means that personal preference is no longer the foundation of love. We love, not because we prefer the beloved, but because God loves the beloved and commands that we imitate his love.

Here is the true ground of the possibility of benevolence. As long as the beloved is primarily an object of my choice, an ego-centric agenda is a constant possibility. But when my primary object of love is God, and I imitate God in my love, then disinterested benevolence becomes the absolute norm. The former beloved of ego-centric preference becomes the beloved of divine commandment. In preferential love the self comes first; in the imitation of Christ God comes first.

In so outlining the dynamics of love for others on the religious level, Kierkegaard has given a clear analysis of the real possibility of benevolence. True benevolence is possible only when God is loved first; all else is gibberish. Every attempt to defend a "natural" benevolence which is not based on God's love and the human imitation of it is doomed to fail, for the self which does not relate to itself through the power which constitutes it is in despair. But when God's love, which is the source of all love, unites the self in the image of God, a new possibility emerges.

It is integral to Kierkegaard's presentation that self, God, and others are not commensurate objects of love. It can never be denied that it is a self who loves, and that the love of self is assumed in all love. Similarly the choice of God or other human being as an object of love is not in conflict, for the self was made to love God first and others through his love. When a self attempts to love God _and_ others, it fails to do both, for God is not one beloved to be chosen among others. Thus in Kierkegaard's presentation the love of self, God, and others is not seen as a conflict if the divinely intended order of love is preserved.

Finally we take up the category of love as judgment and evaluate its applicability to Kierkegaard's description of love on the religious level. We recall that in Hazo's format love may come from a non-cognitive inclination to act or from a cognitive judgment concerning the beloved. On the aesthetic and ethical levels, love is depicted as the former. But on the religious level we see both. The inclination to reach out to God in love is a non-cognitive tendency, loving God for the sustaining grade which completes our incompleteness. But in God's love for us and in our love for others cognitive aspects are seen.

In God's love this is seen in the valuing of humanity even though the value is extrinsic, is imputed by God's love rather than discovered in humanity itself. God's love does not find value; it creates value by benevolently completing our incompleteness.

In human love for others Kierkegaard argues that God should be the middle term and that one loves by the commandment to love. This means that love does not arise from our inner tendencies, but from our understanding and response to commandment. Love here has a cognitive love.

At various points we have mentioned the need for love to be transformed in order to fulfill the criteria which Kierkegaard and his pseudonyms demanded of it. We now see another part of what is involved in this transformation: the integration of the intellect. We have moved from the fragmented existence where self does not relate to self and where the intensity of love is threatened by reflection, to the place where the gulf between cognitive and the non-cognitive modes of consciousness is bridged. As an act of Christian faithfullness it is possible to love God with all our heart and soul and mind and strength, and through loving God love our neighbor as our selves.

Thus the vision of Christian love which Kierkegaard holds up to us is one where love is truly transformed--not the object of love or the intensity of love, but love itself. For the cognitive and non-cognitive factors of love are united by the healing power of God. In presenting this vision, Kierkegaard has kept faith with his mission--to call anyone listening in Christendom to a deeper understanding of God. If one can love in the manner Kierkegaard has described, then true Christian faith has arrived as well.

NOTES
CHAPTER VIII

(1) Nygren, Agape and Eros, pp. 75-81.

(2) Ibid., p. 175.

(3) Denis de Rougemont, Love in the Western World, trans. Montgomery Belgion (New York: Fawcett World Library, 1969), p. 52.

(4) Ibid., pp. 54, 55.

(5) Ibid., p. 57.

(6) Ibid., p. 70.

(7) M.C. D'Arcy, The Mind and Heart of Love (Cleveland, Ohio: The World Publishing Company, 1964), p. 81.

(8) Ibid., p. 48.

(9) Ibid., p. 351.

(10) Ibid., p. 362.

(11) Ibid., p. 354.

(12) Denis de Rougemont, Love in the Western World, p. 321.

(13) Ibid., p. 315.

(14) Søren Kierkegaard, Søren Kierkegaard's Journals and Papers Vol. 3, p. 44.

Chapter IX
Love And Faith
In Kierkegaard

We began this study by pointing out the agenda of the Kierkegaardian corpus: to bring the possibility of real faith into Christendom. In order to do this he sought to find a technique of indirect communication, a way to lead individuals to the realization of their lack of faith without tripping their defenses. This involved sharing how a part of universal experience, love, changes as people move from one level of existence to another. By seeing the kind of love which characterized their lives, people could also see the level of existence on which they lived, and by this reflection might be prompted to move into faith.

Since Kierkegaard was convinced that most people did not know the meaning of true faith (yet thought that they did), he had to find a concept which paralleled faith and could be used as the paradigm for it. Since faith and love are both "passions," the more familiar passion could be used to provide understanding for the less familiar passion. Thus the aesthetic and ethical levels are explored through descriptions of love, and as Kierkegaard takes up the more direct communication of discussing faith, he constantly tells stories of love. Because Kierkegaard is convinced that people know nothing of faith but something of love, love becomes the model to explain faith.

By this correlation of faith and love, two central facts about Kierkegaard's writings are connected: his well-known agenda of introducing a fresh and more radical understanding of faith into Christendom, and the exploration in this study of the wide scope of his writngs on love. The familiar explains the unfamiliar; the known passion of love is the model to understand the unknown passion of faith.

Without attempting to sort through the whole discussion of the adequacy of Kierkegaard's concept of faith, we would conclude this study by commending its results to that discussion, for surely it can now be seen that any investigation of Kierkegaard's concept of faith must have recourse to his notion of love.

Two sections in the Kierkegaardian corpus are crucial in bringing together the concepts of faith and love. The first is the exploration of Abraham's faith in Fear and Trembling. In this writing by an aesthetic pseudonym, Abraham is able to make the double movement of believing that

God required the life of Isaac while trusting that Isaac would yet be the heir of the covenant. There is no way that these may be rationally harmonized. Yet Abraham believed "by virtue of the absurd."

The second section, appearing in Concluding Unscientific Postscript, is the definition of truth as subjectivity and of faith as risk.

Here is such a definition of truth: An objective uncertainty held fast in an appropriation-process of the most passionate inwardness is the truth, the highest truth attainable for an existing individual. At the point where the way swings off (and where this cannot be specified objectively, since it is a matter of subjectivity), there objective knowledge is placed in abeyance. (1)

This definition of truth has a related definition for faith:

Without risk there is no faith. Faith is precisely the contradiction between the infinite passion of the individual's inwardness and the objective uncertainty. If I am capable of grasping God objectively, I do not believe, but precisely because I cannot do this I must believe. (2)

A number of thinkers find fault with Kierkegaard at this point. Arthur Murphy, for example, contends that the leap of faith has no risk if the truth has no objectivity. Kierkegaard presumes objective truth while attacking it:

The point I wish to make is that while it ostensibly turns away from the issue of objective truth, Kierkegaard's procedure presupposes such truth at every step in its retreat into recessive inwardness. His subjectivity is parasitic for its 'existential' significance on the assumed objective truth of a doctrine about man and God whose right to claim such truth it strives at every point to discredit. Not only does it bite the hand that feeds it but it calls this questionable procedure faith. (3)

Two factors are vitally important in evaluating Kierkegaard's ability to withstand such criticism. The first is to remember that these sections are ascribed to pseudonyms. Johannes de silentio is on the aesthetic level, and Johannes Climacus, although fitting best on the religious level, cannot be assumed to speak directly for Kierkegaard either. Kierkegaard's concept of faith must not be equated literally with either of these. Indeed, Concluding Unscientific Postscript has been understood as a parody: A Hegelian attempt to state Kierkegaard's position. (4) Rather, we must remember to interpret the pseudonymous statements about faith in light of Kierkegaard's use of the pseudonym--an indirect communication challenging the reader to identify his or her lack of faith and increase the commitment to Christ. Thus the pseudonymous statements are not offered as definitions of faith, but as descriptions leading to the discovery of the lack of faith.

We have seen how Kierkegaard identified the problem of his age as a lack of passion in faith. Commitment to Christ was popularly identified as verbal assent and occasional participation in Christianity. Intellectual activity was seen by Kierkegaard to be an avoidance of commitment. In the midst of one set of people who identified passion with aesthetic immediacy and another set who identified passion with married commitment, Kierkegaard's pseudonyms described faith as a passion. The message seems to be: take the dynamic which you claim to understand and test your faith by it. By the understanding which you claim, your faith becomes objectively incomprehensible.

It would be a valid question to ask what authentically Kierkegaardian statement on faith could be extrapolated for another age and setting. This, however, is beyond the scope of the present inquiry. However, having recognized the importance of the pseudonyms on that question, we also want to channel the fruit of this study toward an understanding of faith, for it is our claim that the concept of faith in Kierkegaard's writings is best understood with reference to his presentation of love. This is the second of the crucial factors mentioned above.

We cannot be reminded too strongly that, whatever else faith may be, it is for Kierkegaard a passion. As we have seen, in passion the desires of the self confront the obstacle to their fulfillment in such a way that suffering leads to transformation. The intensity of the desire is matched by the intractability of the obstacle. The extent of the suffering dictates the extent of the transformation. If a person claims to be passionate but the desire is weak, the obstacle insignificant, the suffering is minimal, and the transformation inconsequential, we would hardly respect the claim of passion. If a person claims to have faith, but lacks any strong feeling, has no obstacle to overcome and no suffering to bear, and is not changed, we would likewise question the claim of faith. For faith operates by the dynamic of passion.

In the passion of faith the desire is for the eternal happiness of the self through relationship with God. This is in response to the love of God as seen in God's own passionate faithfulness. As a passionate lover, God has encountered the obstacle of the infinite qualitative distinction between the human and the divine, and has overcome it through his incarnation, suffering, and death. This passionate faithfullness in God is symbolized most clearly in the story of the king and the maiden. By moving into the context of our lives in time and space in Jesus Christ, the eternal one has shown his love and initiated the possibility of our loving response.

But an obstacle still remains. How shall we understand and appropriate the activity of the eternal God in our frame of reference? How can we be certain God loves us, since he has loved us by the incarnation and the cross in ways which were so unexpected? That the love of God is so benevolent in its context and transcendent in its source poses a difficulty for our response. It is only by the most intense passion that we may appropriate this reality.

He who with the greatest possible passionateness, in distressful concern for his eternal happiness, is or should be interested in the fact that somebody or another existed, must be interested in the least detail, and yet he cannot attain more than an approximate certainty, and is absolutely in contradiction. (5)

As Johannes Climacus points out in discussing contemporaneity with Christ, faith is required whether we are eye-witnesses to Jesus' life on earth or disciples second hand. Our faith is made certain neither by first hand experience nor the long term experience of the church. Only by the passion of faith do we know with the intense immediacy which our spirit demands. For, as Paul Holmer points out, contemporaneity with Christ is for Kierkegaard the issue of unreflective immediacy in love raised to the religious level. (6) The quest for faith is to overcome the stumbling block of the inability to believe that God's love is true and certain and has come to us in time and space.

Just as a lover is not satisfied until he or she knows with certainty that love is returned, so faith is not satisfied with degrees of certainty.

There has been much said that is strange, much that is deplorable, much that is revolting about Christianity; but the most stupid thing ever said about it is, that it is to a certain degree true. (7)

As immediacy seeks to banish reflection in aesthetic love, so faith seeks to grasp with certain the reality of God's love. Just as the quest for immediacy may not be resolved in aesthetic love by objective certainty, so in the quest for faith the objective is insufficient. Only the subjectivity of passion which confronts the obstacle to certainty and suffers unto transformation can accomplish the goal of faith. For faith is a passion.

It is a real question whether we should consider faith a happy or unhappy love. From the standpoint of Johannes de silentio, faith is a happy love, for in it the knight of faith not only retains belief but regains what was lost. Yet in the Journals, Kierkegaard himself states that loving God makes people unhappy. There are two aspects to this unhappiness: (1) that, judged by earthly standards, God's love is so transcendent as to appear sometimes not to be love at all, and (2) that loving God requires passion, and this, as we have seen, includes suffering. How can we resolve this apparent conflict between Kierkegaard and his pseudonym on this matter?

The motif of unhappy love does not have a complete view of the passion and transformation which can follow. Unhappy love sees only its unhappiness, and it is of this unhappiness that Kierkegaard warned (himself) in his journals. The transformation which follows the passion of love of God is still unhappy by the standards of the world, for the lover cannot repose in the tangibility of the responding love of the beloved. Yet to one whose consciousness has been transformed by the passion of faith, the loving of God is a happy passion, for happy in this instance means blessed. Though one has lost the whole world, in faith one has regained the whole world through the love of the Sovereign of the whole world. In his Journals, then, Kierkegaard warns himself not to be swayed by the world's preliminary view of the happiness of faith, for the real understanding of the happiness of the passion of faith lies in beatitude.

Having seen then how Kierkegaard used the notion of love to lead people indirectly to examine their lives and perhaps come to faith, and having seen how the passion of faith operates in a parallel manner to the passion of love, we turn again to the charge that Kierkegaard's concept of faith is irrational. And freely we would admit the validity of the charge if faith is a kind of knowledge. But if faith is a passion, and if the purpose of Kierkegaard's pseudonyms is to intensify the obstacle of passion in order to magnify the transformation of passion, then the question of rationality should be put another way. Instead of asking "Is the notion of faith articulated by the pseudonyms rational? we should ask: "How do the paradoxical statements of faith relate to the process and sequence of transformation?" "What is the logic of transformation?"

Hegelian logic posited the coming to consciousness in history through a sequence of thesis-antithesis-synthesis. Kierkegaard posited the coming to the highest consciousness of faith through desire, passionate suffering, and transformation. In place of the immediacy of aesthetic love, faith offers the immediacy of contemporaneity with Christ.

In this sequence paradox is a rationalist perspective of the obstacle, serving to intensify the passion. Surely Abraham must have struggled with the three questions of the problemata presented in Fear and Trembling, recognizing that the wisdom of the world would lead him away from obedience to the voice he heard. Surely Abraham realized that the demand for Isaac's sacrifice and the promise of Isaac's posterity could not be reconciled rationally. Abraham's dilemma, then, was to have faith in the promise of Isaac's posterity while at the same time ending the possibility of that posterity through an act of faith in the sacrifice of Isaac. In the dilemma, up against the obstacle of the paradox, consciousness is transformed and the sacrifice is provided by God. Seen from the perspective of faith, God is faithful and is able to do all things. In Abraham's passion consciousness is transformed and God's promise is fulfilled.

Just as in the sequence of Hegel's logic thesis is opposed by antithesis and they are combined in synthesis, in Kierkegaard's logic of faith, consciousness is heightened by the encounter with the obstacle of faith. Through suffering comes the understanding of God's faithfullness. The charge of irrationalism misses the point, treats penultimate as ultimate. What is irrational in the world's understanding is presented to lead to a fresh perception of the wisdom of God.

Thus the dynamics of the passion of love leads us to understand the passion of faith. But we also remember that Kierkegaard's challenge was to more than the understanding. It is my hope, therefore, that those who read this direct communication about love have also found the occassion to examine their own lives and loves, as have I. If Kierkegaard is right in believing that exploring love deepens faith, let us ever set our course to chart these endless depths.

NOTES
CHAPTER IX

(1) Søren Kierkegaard, Concluding Unscientific Postscript, p. 182.

(2) Ibid.

(3) Arthur Murphy, "On Kierkegaard's Claim that 'Truth is Subjectivity'," in Essays on Kierkegaard ed. Jerry Gill (Minneapolis, Minn.: Burgess Publishing Company, 1969), p. 99.

(4) Henry Allison, "Christianity and Nonsense," in Essays on Kierkegaard ed. Jerry Gill (Minneapolis, Minn.: Burgess Publishing Co., 1969), p. 127.

(5) Søren Kierkegaard, Concluding Unscientific Postscript, p. 511.

(6) Paul Holmer, "On Understanding Kierkegaard" in A Kierkegaardian Critique ed. Howard Johnson and Niels Thulstrup (New York; Harper and Brothers, 1962), p. 47.

(6) Søren Kierkegaard, Concluding Unscientific Postscript, p. 205.

SELECTED BIBLIOGRAPHY ON KIERKEGAARD AND LOVE

Works by Kierkegaard

The Concept of Dread. trans. with intro. by Walter Lowrie, Princeton: Princeton University Press, 1970.

Concluding Unscientific Postscript. trans. David Swenson, intro. by Walter Lowrie. Princeton: Princeton University Press, 1968.

Christian Discourses and the Lilies of the Field and the Birds of the Air and Three Discourses at the Communion on Fridays. trans. with introduction by Walter Lowrie. Princeton: Princeton University Press, 1971.

Either/Or I. trans. David and Lillian Swenson. Garden City, New York: Doubleday nd Company, 1959.

Either/Or I. trans. Walter Lowrie. Garden City, New York: Doubleday and Company, 1959.

Fear and Trembling/Sickness Unto Death. trans. with intro. by Walter Lowrie. Garden City, New York: Doubleday and Company, 1954.

Philosophical Fragments. trans. with commentary by Howard Hong. Princeton: Princeton University Press, 1971.

The Point of View for My Work as An Author: A Report to History. trans. with intro. by Walter Lowrie, ed. Benjamin Nelson. New York: Harper and Row, 1962.

The Present Age. trans. Alexander Dru with intro. by Walter Kaufmann. New York: Harper and Row, 1952.

Repetition: An Essay in Experimental Psychology. trans. with intro. by Walter Lowrie, New York: Harper and Row, 1964.

Søren Kierkegaard's Journals and Papers Vol. 3. ed. and trans. by Howard and Edna Hong. Bloomington and London: Indiana University Press, 1975.

Stages on Life's Way. trans. Walter Lowrie with intro. by Paul Sponheim. New York: Schocken Books, 1967.

Works of Love. trans. Howard and Edna Hong. New York: Harper and Row, 1964.

Works on Kierkegaard

Allison, Henry, "Christianity and Nonsense," in Essays on Kierkegaard, ed.
Jerry Gill. Minneapolis, Minn.: Burgess Publishing Co., 1969.

Collins, James. The Mind of Kierkegaard. Chicago: Henry Regnery Co.,
1967.

Grimsley, Ronald. Søren Kierkegaard and French Literature. Cardiff:
University of Wales Press, 1966.

Holmer, Paul, "On Understanding Kierkegaard," in A Kierkegaardian
Critique, ed. Howard Johnson and Niels Thulstrup. New York; Harper
and Brothers, Publishers, 1962.

Mackey, Louis. Kierkegaard: A Kind of Poet. Philadelphia: University of
Philadelphia Press, 1972.

Murphy, Aurthur, "On Kierkegaard's Claim that 'Truth is Subjectivity'," in
Essays on Kierkegaard, ed. Jerry Gill. Minneapolis, Minn.: Burgess
Publishing Co., 1969.

Works on Love

D'Arcy, M.C. The Mind and Heart of Love. Cleveland, Ohio: World
Publishing Company, 1964.

Grabbe, Christian Dietrich. Don Juan and Faust. Leipzig: G. Wigard, 1909.

Hazo, Robert. The Idea of Love, Concepts in Western Thought Series, ed.
Mortimer Adler. New York; Frederick A. Praeger, Publishers, 1967.

Nygren, Anders. Agape and Eros. Trans. by Philip Watson, Philadelphia:
The Westminster Press ,1953.

de Rougemont, Denis. Love in the Western World. Trans. by Montgomery
Belgion. New York: Fawcett World Library, 1969.

Other Works Cited

The Encyclopedia of Philosophy, reprint ed. S.v. "Romanticism" by Crane
Brinton.

Vinterberg, Hermann, and Bodelsen, C.A.   Dansk-Engelsk Ordbog.
Kobenhavn: Glydendalske Boghandel, 1954.